Action Learning Guide

Action Learning Guide: Real Learning, Real Results

Claudia Hill

H. Skipton Leonard, Ph.D.

Marc B. Sokol, Ph.D.

PDI PERSONNEL DECISIONS INTERNATIONAL
REAL LEADERSHIP ADVANTAGE™

North America • Europe • Asia Pacific

Australia • Middle East • Latin America

www.personneldecisions.com

Contents

Introduction

Action Learning Gaining Popularity

Organizations across the world are increasing their use of Action Learning for several reasons. The pace of change requires more efficient skill mastery techniques. Action Learning fosters boundary-spanning relationships. Perhaps most important, the Action Learning process can lead to real answers to tough problems.

The Potential of Action Learning

In many organizations, learning is incidental as task forces work on issues or reengineer processes. Rotational assignments provide meaningful development experiences, but they are largely focused on individuals. Team building enables groups to learn together and work more effectively, but it doesn't necessarily address issues that challenge organizations across boundaries. Action Learning has the potential to unleash types of learning seldom available to employees.

Personnel Decisions International (PDI) Approach to Action Learning

Our approach in this guide is practical and proven; it has been developed and used in our client work, and in the work of other Action Learning practitioners.

Our practical view of the Action Learning process begins with three core principles:

- We believe there is a need to see Action Learning as an end-to-end process, which starts with the decision to use this approach and culminates with the presentation and evaluation of a team's recommendations.
- We believe there is value in not only recognizing the role of Sponsors, but in engaging them to maximize the impact of their role.
- We believe Learning Coaches discipline themselves to focus on critical reflection instead of employing conventional means of team facilitation.

Is This Book for You?

The Personnel Decisions International Action Learning Guide is written for and by people who are currently working with Action Learning methodology in organizations around the world.

We give you details about Action Learning roles and the process. Whether you are a Program Manager, Business Issue Sponsor, Team Member, or Learning Coach, you will find information tailored to you.

Navigating the Book

We designed the book around our Action Learning process, depicted here:

Chapters contain practical tools, models, and examples for each step in the process. In the final chapter, we address Action Learning in an organizational context, describing methods for embedding the approach as an integral part of the way people work and learn.

The GPI Story

Throughout the book, we tell the story of Eric Svenson, who is implementing Action Learning at his company, Global Products International (GPI).

Eric represents the experiences of many of our clients as they go through the process of selecting Action Learning, planning the implementation, selecting Sponsors and teams, working through the issues, and delivering presentations.

As you read Eric's story, apply his questions and experiences to your situation. Would Action Learning fit the learning needs of your organization?

Join Us in Action Learning

As you implement Action Learning in your organization, we invite you to share your experiences with us. Your questions, stories, and feedback will enrich the conversation and help us learn together. After all, isn't that the goal?

Email us at moreinfo@personneldecisions.com.

1

What Is Action Learning?

Global Products International (GPI), a manufacturer of vehicle parts, is a widely admired global leader. Much of their success is due to their employees, who value continuous learning and recognize that it is the key to creating a compelling future for themselves and the firm. Accordingly, GPI offers a range of leadership development programs, managed both by the Corporate Development Center in New Jersey and by Regional Directors.

Eric Svenson is the Regional Director for Learning and Development in EMEA (Europe, Middle East, and Africa), GPI's fastest growing market. He needs country managers who can address issues that cut across product lines and markets. One issue they face is competition and rivalry between business units, especially GPI Vehicles and GPI Marine. Both sell the same components; however, GPI Marine has become more profitable, especially in Southern Europe. A second issue involves product quality concerns, which surface more quickly in the vehicle business line. Underlying both issues is inconsistent communication between business lines.

Due to the fierce competition for talent in his region, Eric knows that the majority of country managers will need to be developed from within the organization. Looking at his mid-level talent pool, including product directors and senior managers, Eric recognizes that individuals are very good at what they do, but there is a big gap between the challenges of their current roles and those of country managers. Talented as these leaders are, they're only responsible for a single product line or market. Before they can move into a country leader assignment, they need to broaden their capabilities. They also need to learn how to work with other high-potential leaders. Currently, the competitive spirit that drives them to excellence in their own areas inhibits their ability to build relationships across product and business lines.

Eric has heard about Action Learning and wonders whether it will give him an opportunity both to develop talent at this level and address some of the more challenging issues that confront the region. For example, GPI wants to recruit the best engineers early in their careers. Also, Eric knows that senior leaders want to see more communication across business and product groups, and a more supportive environment in which this can occur. Communication won't improve simply by telling people to act differently.

To learn more about Action Learning, Eric attends a conference, reads several articles, and talks with two colleagues at other firms who share their experiences with Action learning, both positive and negative. Eric's research convinces him to try Action Learning. He puts together a list of elements that he will need for a successful Action Learning experience:
- An engaging process that appeals to high-potential leaders and sustains their motivation over time
- A process to ensure the right people participate
- A plan to prevent Action Learning from being misused for other agendas
- Support from key sponsors, including managers of the participants and higher level executives
- Extremely challenging projects that participants find credible and that add value to the organization

- A way to address the costs of involving participants from Europe, the Middle East, and Africa
- A clear process to initiate Action Learning and take it forward
- A group of coaches, consultants, and facilitators to support the teams during the process

GPI has many of the right conditions for a successful Action Learning initiative. It also has a list of fundamental questions.

- What is Action Learning?
- What makes it work?
- What is the value of Action Learning to an organization?

We will address these initial questions in this chapter and follow Global Product International's experiences with Action Learning at each phase of the process.

What Is Action Learning?

*A*ction Learning is a process for working on challenging problems that helps people develop skills, fosters learning communities, and contributes to the creation of an agile, competitive, organization.

Action Learning offers organizations a structured opportunity to deal with real, challenging business issues while improving team and individual effectiveness. It delivers fresh ideas for tough problems. In many organizations it has become an important vehicle for development. For example, Action Learning is a rite of passage in long-standing, high-potential learning systems like those at Boeing, Anheuser-Busch, and General Electric.

Action Learning is simple; so simple it can be hard to define. Victoria Marsick, a leading expert in organizational learning, explains it as an approach to working with people.

"Action Learning is an approach to working with and developing people that uses work on an actual project or problem as the way to learn. Participants work in small groups to take action to solve their problem and learn how to learn from action."

Yorks, O'Neil, & Marsick, 2000

Key Figures in the Historical Development of Action Technologies

In 1946, German psychologist Kurt Lewin and his associates began to address the problems that prevent effective discussion in groups. Lewin championed the use of an Action Research approach, a form of inquiry that required a closer involvement of the researcher and what was researched. Action research evolved as a way to systematically study human social behavior. This closer relationship and emphasis on action created the theoretical foundation for work by Reg Revans and Chris Argyris.

> ### Chris Argyris and Action Science
>
> *When individuals engage in double-loop learning, they explore the assumptions behind actions and interactions. Most Learning Coaches employ an Action Science approach as they work with teams.*

Reg Revans, a physicist, researcher, and scholar, developed the term Action Learning to describe the learning behaviors of people he observed at work, from coal miners to physicians. He observed the impact of collegial interactions in scientific laboratories on both the results achieved and knowledge acquired, and later created the same sorts of conditions with managers in the British coal mines after World War II (Marquardt, 1999). Since Reg Revans' time, Action Learning increasingly has been used in a wide variety of organizations to develop leadership capacity.

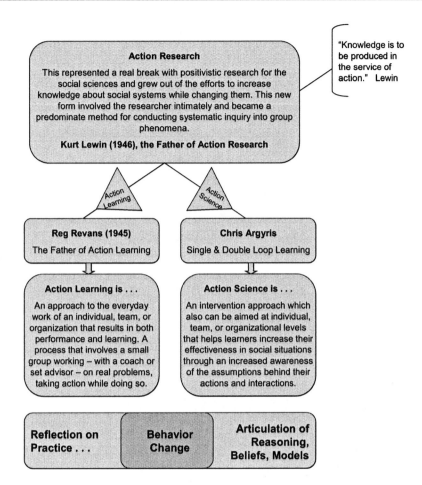

Action Learning Is Not Training

Action Learning is often used to develop people in organizations, but it's not a training program. Action Learning differs from training in several ways:

- The interaction of performance and learning are different. Experts agree that Action Learning seeks to improve learning through performance; traditional training seeks to improve performance through learning.

- Learning goals are not predetermined in Action Learning. In Action Learning, the needs of individual team members and the demands of the project determine the learning objectives. In traditional training, the program design specifies learning objectives.
- Action Learning is not driven by a predetermined agenda. In a sense, the agenda of an Action Learning group is set by the questions they pursue on their journey through the problem-solving process.
- A Learning Coach is a catalyst, not a subject matter expert. A Learning Coach is not an expert in anything but process and learning. The Learning Coach is expected to provide helpful questions at key junctures. All participants are expected to contribute ideas and employ critical thinking to challenge assumptions.

An Action Learning Team Is Not a Task Force

Although real work tasks are at the heart of Action Learning, an Action Learning team is not a task force. Here are some ways they differ:

- A task force has one clear objective; an Action Learning team has several. For example, an Action Learning team might bring new insight to old issues, reflect on attempted solutions, challenge long-held assumptions, and develop team members.
- Challenging assumptions is a large part of the Action Learning process, which takes time. In a task force, urgency and deadlines are often the primary drivers. The focus on completing the task is so strong that questioning the basic reasons for undertaking the task or the assumptions that make the task relevant can be unwelcome. Conversely, in Action Learning, challenging assumptions allows people to change how they solve problems, leading to evolutionary, adaptive approaches. If an Action Learning team reaches a quick solution, they may miss the lessons available from the inquiry process.
- Action Learning initiatives emphasize reflection. This process of thinking about actions and decisions is the heart of Action Learning.

What Makes Action Learning Work

You may be asking, "If Action Learning is not a training program or a task force initiative, then how exactly does it work?"

Action Learning is an approach to work (action) that includes time for questions (learning). Revans proposed that the core of Action Learning can be expressed by the equation $L = P + Q$, where learning [L] occurs through programmed knowledge [P] and insightful questioning [Q] (Revans 1982).

Action Learning interrupts the usual approach to solving business problems with a focus on reflection and new thinking. It is generally consistent with what is known about individual learning. For example, when teams try different solutions, this offers opportunities to learn — if they pay attention to them.

> *"Action Learning is an approach to the everyday work of an individual, team, or organization that results in both performance and learning, a process that involves a small group working on real problems in real time, taking action, and learning while doing so."*
>
> *Yorks, O'Neil & Marsick (2000)*

Organizational Context for Action Learning

The Action Learning process works well in a full range of organizational environments, including global corporations such as General Electric, Ford Motor Company, and Hewlett-Packard, government and non-government organizations, university business school programs, and community-based organizations.

When you engage in Action Learning as a participant, you consciously work your way through an entire learning cycle (Kolb 1984). First, you identify a problem or challenge you are experiencing, then you work with a team to reflect and review what has already been done. Next, you conceptualize by interpreting the events. Finally you plan what you want to do.

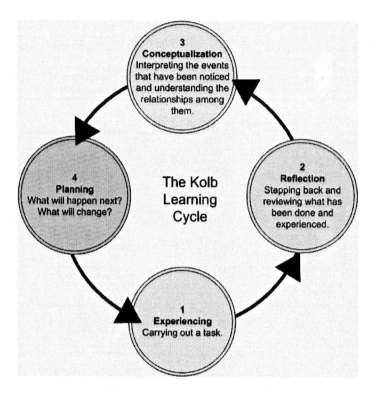

At its best, Action Learning stresses the value of disciplined problem solving, generalization, and reflection to bring about insight on serious issues.

Reflection, conscious theory building, and disciplined theory testing with further analysis gives Action Learning its power to both develop people and solve real problems. From a diagnostic point of view, the greater the pace of business and change in a given organization, the greater the potential impact of Action Learning.

Action Learning Components

Business Issue

One of the most critical components of Action Learning is the business issue. A successful business issue is identified by team members and organizational sponsors, and is both compelling and engaging. The organization either assigns a business issue to an Action Learning team or the team selects a problem that the organization finds important. Preferably, the issue is one that has resisted solution by conventional means.

The team frames the problem and identifies which organizational outcomes could result from a new approach. They interview senior managers affected by the problem to gather facts about the severity and cost or opportunity the problem presents. The team needs to sell its approach to senior managers to gain sponsorship for the effort. Also, they need to forge a relationship with at least one senior mentor who can guide the team through the political implications of the problem.

Sponsorship

A Business Issue Sponsor is an organizational leader who agrees to support Action Learning, the project, and/or support the team. Sponsorship support is an important factor in Action Learning success. Executive Panel members select or approve issues, Business Issue Sponsors provide access to resources, attend group sessions (particularly the launch

> ## Business Issue Examples
>
> *Improve leadership communication*
> An Action Learning team at a high-technology firm studied the link between change initiatives, communication from leaders, morale, and turnover.
>
> *Improve processes*
> An Action Learning team investigated usage patterns of financial reports at a professional services firm.
>
> *Improve marketing*
> An Action Learning team developed a new point of purchase display system for big-box retail organizations.

session), and work with the Learning Coach to hold their team accountable for both action and learning. Program Managers design, implement, and maintain momentum in Action Learning.

The Action Learning Team

Action Learning teams might be intact work teams or they might be new teams drawn from across the organization, which optimizes networking across organizational boundaries. Typically, Action Learning teams comprise approximately eight leaders from different job functions and geographical regions. At regularly scheduled meetings, the team analyzes the problem from many angles, performs a systematic causal analysis, and makes practical recommendations to senior management. Simultaneously, the team learns how to approach problems in a new way and realizes the value of reflective thinking. They establish strong and lasting bonds with each other. Action Learning teams might also take part in implementing the recommended solutions or monitoring the benefits to the organization, as jointly defined with senior management early in the discovery phase.

Commitment to Learning

The team sets and monitors its learning and project goals. If the commitment to learning is low, or if the team views involvement as a medium priority or an optional activity, Action Learning will fail.

Action and Outcomes

Unlike a training program or a simulation, Action Learning requires participants to produce a real result, which involves taking action. One of the keys to success for Action Learning is an upfront identification of the expected outcomes and required levels of action.

Questioning and Reflection

During Action Learning meetings, participants are required to ask questions, challenge thinking, and uncover new ideas. Following the meeting, a Learning Coach might facilitate a session in which participants reflect and capture learning.

Learning Coach

Action Learning teams require a specially skilled coach who can set up and keep the process optimized for both problem solving and learning. The coach keeps the group focused on organizational learning insights and personal development. He or she also helps the team surface assumptions about what they learn, encourages them to challenge inconsistencies, and points out opportunities to reflect and learn from the discovery and problem-solving process.

What Is the Value of Action Learning to an Organization?

Experience generates learning throughout our lives. In fact, most of what we learn as adults comes through what we experience. Take a moment to reflect:

- Which experiences in the past month had a great impact on you?
- What did you learn from these experiences?
- How will this learning change you as you go forward?

Without reflection and conscious thought, a lot of what we learn through experience remains unused. However, acknowledged or not, exploited or not, this type of learning goes on throughout our lifetimes. It's part of what makes us adaptive and successful.

Groups of people and whole organizations can collaborate to learn in much the same way. The problem is, they often don't. Organizations need collaborative learning to implement strategy and remain competitive. Regardless of careful planning, the reality is that most organizations cannot predict where marketplace forces will take them. Rapidly evolving technology, globalization, and the sheer pace of change means that knowledge and skills that are valuable today may quickly become obsolete. People in organizations need an efficient and effective method for collaborating and learning from experience. They need well-designed Action Learning.

Action Learning and the PDI Development Pipeline®

The PDI Development Pipeline® represents the necessary and sufficient elements within a learning system that speed the pace and increase the sustained impact of development efforts. PDI's Action Learning process has the potential to develop people along the entire pipeline.

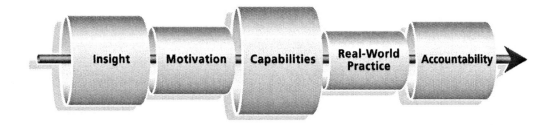

Insight ▪ Motivation ▪ Capabilities ▪ Real-World Practice ▪ Accountability ➤

Insight

People must clearly understand the effectiveness of their behavior. The process of reflection in Action Learning makes learning explicit, leading to greater awareness and insight. Participants learn to use questions, such as, "Is this all you want here?" and "What is the purpose?" When Action Learning focuses on real business problems and on areas where people are stuck, participants can identify which behaviors and assumptions are pivotal to improve results.

Motivation

For sustained action, a person engaged in self-development must be motivated. When people work on projects that are highly significant to the organization and to themselves, motivation comes naturally. Action Learning provides an opportunity to learn, gain visibility, and make an impact within the organization.

Capabilities

People need to know how and where they can acquire new capabilities. By definition, Action Learning teams should have both a learning agenda and a task agenda. New capabilities are learned through experimentation, reflection, feedback, and just-in-time coaching. Learning can be integrated with real work.

Real-World Practice

People need opportunities to apply what they have learned. Within the context of an Action Learning process, participants apply what they learn to solve their central problem. This alone does not guarantee that learning will be applied elsewhere. Transfer of learning is easier when the learning task is a real issue and there is organizational support for integrating learning with work.

Accountability

Does development have a positive impact on performance? Accountability is strong if there are real consequences connected to the outcomes of the program. Establishing clear objectives and a process to evaluate outcomes builds accountability.

2

Is Action Learning the Right Approach?

"This can be a great opportunity for you and GPI, Eric," enthused Alberto Meroni, Eric's colleague at Amalfi Industries. "I have used the Action Learning approach twice, and have great appreciation for its value. But let me tell you, my first time as Program Manager was nearly a disaster! You know that old saying, 'Vision without action is a dream, action without vision is a nightmare?' Well, we had a short-lived dream followed by a lengthy nightmare!"

"What do you mean?" laughed Eric.

"I hadn't really thought through what we were trying to do, so I didn't know when to push back when other agendas began to show up," explained Alberto. "I wasn't able to orchestrate the action in a consistent direction, so we had teams doing everything, thinking they could rebuild the company!"

"What did you do?" asked Eric.

"Fortunately, my executive committee had the presence of mind to see that this was a good idea that was not being implemented properly. We put the

15

> projects on hold, got some sound advice on how to structure what we wanted to do, and restarted the process nine months later. Action Learning is great, but you actively have to create the magic!"
>
> After Eric hung up the telephone, he added two more items to his list on how to do Action Learning well.
> • As Program Manager, clearly define the intended scope of the project.
> • Identify who will set the boundaries for the type of projects to consider and who will ultimately approve them.

In this chapter we discuss one of the most critical questions Program Managers must address as they consider Action Learning: "Is this the right approach?" We provide a decision tree to help you think through the pros and cons. Our intent is to offer a realistic preview of what it takes to do Action Learning well and what can go wrong. We describe several examples that lead to the success or failure of the Action Learning process. This will increase the odds that if you choose Action Learning, you can do so successfully and with confidence in the process.

Action Learning Addresses Important Organizational Challenges

Action Learning is not appropriate for every learning need, but it can be an important component of an organization's overall development strategy. For many organizations around the world, Action Learning has become one of the most powerful action-oriented, problem-solving tools as well as their key approach to individual, team, and organizational development.

Here are some reasons organizations choose Action Learning:
• Build the ability to work collaboratively across boundaries with a team of colleagues.

- Develop leadership and team skills.
- Provide real-time, effective peer feedback.
- Improve capacity to learn while addressing a real business issue.
- Discover new ways of working.
- Broaden knowledge of other functions, businesses, and external environment.
- Deliver a value-added outcome to the organization by having a team work on engaging business issues not currently being addressed.

Michael Marquardt explains that Action Learning has the unique and inherent capability of being simultaneously applied to the five most pressing needs facing organizations today (Marquardt, 2005 SIOP Presentation):

- Problem solving. Action Learning can help people in organizations find solutions to complex problems.
- Organizational learning. Action Learning can be seen as a form of organizational learning. Action Learning teams serve as a model and an impetus for individual, group, and company-wide learning.
- Team building. Action Learning helps develop strong teams and build skills for individuals to work effectively on future teams.
- Leadership development. Action Learning has become the premier way for training current and future managers throughout the world because it prepares and develops leaders to deal with real problems.
- Professional growth and career development. High levels of self-awareness, self-development, and continuous learning are gained via Action Learning.

When Is Action Learning Most Appropriate? Not Appropriate?

A learning solution flexible enough to address so many diverse needs is very appealing and can generate a lot of interest and preliminary support. Yet, the choice to engage in Action Learning requires a significant investment in time and other resources, so it must be made with care. Program Managers who are considering Action Learning must be able to identify when it is appropriate and when it is not.

Action Learning is most appropriate when:

- There is equal value to be gained by solving business problems and developing individuals and groups for the future.
- An identified gap can be filled by learning, as opposed to a change in the organizational environment.
- The organization supports critical reflection on its norms and assumptions.
- Higher levels of management provide support.

Action Learning is not appropriate when:

- The issue or need to be addressed is simple and straightforward. An appropriate level of challenge is directly related to the potential for learning. The greater the effort, the greater the potential learning.
- The issue or need is pressing and delay is not possible; for example, in emergencies or catastrophes. Action Learning would introduce an unacceptable delay in these instances.
- No expertise exists in the organization to tackle the problem. While a wide diversity of skills makes for a good Action Learning team, relevant and accessible expertise is crucial.
- Managers do not value the opinions of workers or see merit in developing individuals for the future. One of the greatest opportunities of Action Learning is to put the power for action in the hands of the person(s) closest to the issue. Leadership support is fundamental to all aspects of the Action Learning process.
- There is insufficient upper management support. Action Learning requires individuals and teams to take risks for their own growth and organizational development. With support, it's strong medicine. Without support, it's poison.

Is Action Learning the Right Approach?

The following decision tree depicts key decisions and alternatives that should be addressed when considering Action Learning for your organization.

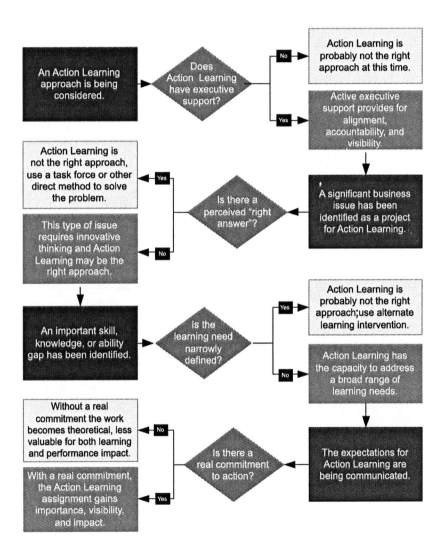

GPI: A Good Match for Action Learning

As a development approach, Action Learning is a good match for GPI's EMEA region. They need to develop cross-boundary thinking in their leaders, who will do this regularly when they move to the next level of leadership. The Action Learning projects have the potential to broaden participants' knowledge of the business and help them learn while addressing real business issues. Plus, the relationship-building potential can have a huge payoff for the participants in the years to come.

Action Learning is a suitable approach, but not the only approach Eric Svenson might have considered. Instead of using Action Learning, which uses a temporary task team, the EMEA region could address these needs through a more permanent redesign of responsibilities, creating formal roles that span markets, functions, or countries.

If Eric used the decision tree, he probably could not answer some of the questions. For example, he doesn't yet know how much executive support there is for Action Learning. Although he has a go-ahead reaction to most of the questions in the decision tree, he might want to explore further before settling on Action Learning.

Eric might want to conduct a Development Systems Review to explore the alignment between strategic priorities and mission to the structure and design of the learning and development function. A Development Systems Review captures the experiences of employees and managers with respect to how well the development function addresses their needs and those of the firm.

This type of review would tell Eric with more certainty what the hopes and needs of the target population are, as well as how their managers view development in the organization. It would shed light on why some initiatives have more sustaining impact than others. A Development Systems Review would ensure broader representation of stakeholders in that understanding. It might also reinforce Eric's plans by highlighting the urgency of creating viable development opportunities, given the gap between the target population and the requirements for successful performance at the next leadership level.

Why Action Learning Fails

The film director Billy Wilder said, "Hindsight is always 20-20." Our experience tells us that there are many reasons why Action Learning can fail. The following checklist may be helpful for you to consider.

Like signposts on a highway, these should not deter you from the journey; rather, they should alert you to the expectations you set for yourself and others. Just as a lengthy journey should begin with a check of what resources will be needed along the way, we offer this list of eight things that can derail the trip, slow it down, or make the journey painful.

Be a well-prepared traveler: take appropriate precautions, ensure you and your passengers are ready for the journey, and avoid common speed traps.

Inappropriate Problem ✓

An inappropriate problem is the single most critical cause of failure. The problem creates the purpose, the urgency, the excitement, and the intensity of effort for action and learning. Problems may be:
• Unimportant, too small, or too simple. The energy and capacity of the group will not be tested. They won't get the best ideas.
• Not real to the organization. Issues and projects need to be genuine, not hypothetical. Otherwise, Action Learning will just be a case study.
• Beyond the authority or scope of the responsibility of the group. This may cause frustration and a sense that the problem will be impossible to solve.

- Too large and complex. This can cause confusion and chaos. The problem may overwhelm rather than invigorate the group.
- Too abstract and not connected to what participants need to learn. This type of problem offers little opportunity for learning or applying learning. Organizations and teams need to select problems that offer the greatest amount of potential learning, which is the long-range benefit of Action Learning.

Lack of Organizational Support ✓

- To be successful, there must be top-level support for the program and for the participants.
- Companies can show support by allowing participation during work hours and by providing space and facilities. Companies should also show keen and immediate support for the actions and solutions generated.

Lack of Time ✓

- Because group meetings cannot be squeezed into an hour here and there, long-range planning is required. Everyone must make a commitment to attend all group meetings.
- Some groups do not allow sufficient time between meetings for members to apply the actions they planned during the meetings. Having actions to reflect on is crucial for Action Learning.
- Some teams do not allow enough time during Action Learning meetings. To assure sufficient time for reflection and learning for each member at each meeting, careful attention must be paid to the clock. Time should also be allocated for assessing the overall meeting.

Poor Mix of Members ✓

- The composition of the team is important. Teams need four to eight members who are committed to the process. This should be an intelligent, strategic mix of individuals, which might come from various parts of the organization, other organizations, the community, customers, and suppliers. The best teams balance gender, age, and learning styles. They include people who will ask naive questions and challenge assumptions.

- In global organizations, Action Learning assignments may allow participants to form relationships and break down barriers with colleagues from around the world. Care should be taken with the formation of these teams. One practical consideration is timing. A team representing many time zones may have difficulty finding convenient times for all team members to meet.

Poor Problem Framing and Problem Solving ✓

- The group may feel constrained to accept, without question, the scope and framework of the problem. This prevents the group from scoping the problem into a manageable size, and framing the problem into a question that can be addressed in light of the team members' capabilities.
- The presenter or group may not be motivated to solve the problem.
- The group may desire a too-quick solution. This means the problem will not receive the necessary reflection, attention, and energy for a high-quality solution.
- A low-quality solution might be acceptable because the problem is low priority.
- Problems that seem familiar often receive a quick fix.
- The group may have little experience in framing and handling challenging problems. The habit of questioning is hard to get into.

Lack of Commitment to Learning ✓

- In many high-performing organizations, Action Learning is launched with full acknowledgement of the importance of both learning and results. However, the focus on learning can fall away due to pressure for results and potential competition between learning teams. What's left is simply a task force.

- Managers, Business Issue Sponsors, Executive Panel members, and Learning Coaches are all in a position to provide accountability; each must operate with the understanding that learning gained by the group has a greater long-term benefit than any short-term result.

Insufficient Commitment ✓

- With insufficient commitment to action and/or inadequate development of action steps, the group may question the importance of the project and of the learning.
- The action plan is a vital element; there is no real learning without action. The plan may lack action steps that specifically describe what will be done by when. Plans should be feasible and progress should be monitored.

Too Much or Too Little Structure that Blocks Progress ✓

- If meetings are not carefully planned, there won't be enough time for problem reframing and for each participant to engage in the process.
- Too much structure can introduce unnecessary protocol, deference to hierarchy, and other formalities.
- Without a designated Learning Coach, the necessary critical reflection will not occur. The Learning Coach maintains the balance between action and learning.

Action Learning Execution Model

If we know what makes Action Learning fail, we also know what makes it succeed. As with anything important, success will follow when vision and execution align. The Action Learning Execution Model presents a proven five-phase approach to implementing Action Learning in organizations.

Phase 1: Organizational Preparation

Business problems and learning needs prompt decision makers to consider an Action Learning approach. During this phase, the organizational infrastructure for Action Learning success is created. Key players are identified: Program Manager, Executive Panel Members, and Business Issue Sponsors. These players work together to identify business issues and determine measures of success.

Phase 2: Team Selection

- This phase completes the organizational preparation begun in Phase 1, and includes the selection and formation of the Action Learning team. During this phase, members of the team are identified and the Learning Coach is selected. There are various methods for selection. To the extent possible, the problem should drive team member selection. In a top-down process, Business Issue Sponsors and the Program Manager should work together to identify the logical mix of people to solve the problem or address the issue.
- During this phase, process education for the team is conducted. In preparation for the next phase, the Action Learning launch event is developed.

Phase 3: Action Learning Teamwork (1)

During this phase, the Action Learning teams are launched and the work of the team begins. Specifically, the teams:
- Clarify understanding of the problem.
- Negotiate the scope of problem with the Business Issue Sponsor.
- Establish norms, logistics, resources, and use of collaboration tools.
- Invest in mission-focused relationship building.
- Set team development goals and identify individual learning goals.
- Are empowered to act and learn.
- Practice critical reflection skills.

Once these initial goals are accomplished, teams move on to directly address the problem. They gather information, evaluate options, develop a concept validation process, and continuously reflect and learn.

The teams meet frequently over several months to review progress, challenge each others' thinking, collect and recognize learning, learn to engage in real dialogue, and dynamically adapt their problem-solving approach to the realities they encounter as they investigate the problem in new ways. These meetings are facilitated by Learning Coaches, who challenge their thinking and lead them toward self-facilitation.

Learning Coaches are skilled at knowing when to get involved in the action of the team. The approach of a Learning Coach reflects the dynamic of the situation and the learning needs of the group.

Phase 4: Action Learning Teamwork (2)

In the previous phase, team members deliberately sought out the broadest possible range of solutions. During this phase, the team moves toward action and as a first step, selects a solution. They use data from the concept validation to prepare a business case, then they prepare a presentation of findings, along with an implementation plan.

Phase 5: Results Assessment

During this phase, the team presents recommendations to the sponsor(s) and seeks approval for further action. Learning and performance results are assessed, and a new issue is selected.

Summary

*A*t this point, you have a high-level appreciation of the Action Learning process and the initial decision criteria on whether or not to go ahead. If you have decided that this is right for you, then it's time to get started.

3

Where Do You Start?

*A*ction Learning has a lot of face validity with organizational decision makers. The notion of learning from everyday work just naturally creates enthusiasm. As one of PDI's clients said, "Who wouldn't get excited about the idea of using teams of motivated employees to solve tough problems, drive improved business results, and generate learning all the while?" In addition to the immediate face validity, the principles of Action Learning are appealingly simple (on the surface) — so simple that in many instances, Business Issue Sponsors rush to implementation and miss important steps along the way. These missed steps can turn initial enthusiasm into equal measures of resistance.

While the necessary elements of Action Learning may be understood, the oversimplification of its implementation can create a new set of problems. As Albert Einstein said, "Everything should be made as simple as possible, but not one bit simpler."

In Chapter 2, the central question was, "Is Action Learning the right approach for my organization?" This chapter begins with the assumption that your answer to the previous question was, "You bet it's the right approach! How do I get started?" and focuses on Phase I of Action Learning: preparing the organization.

29

Action Learning as an Organizational Development Intervention

*A*t PDI, we see Action Learning as an organizational development intervention. Most purely educational interventions target some kind of transactional organizational change. In contrast, Action Learning aims for transformational change in the way people work.

Action Learning has transformational goals. The first involves changes in the way people work together and drive for results. In many organizations, the pace and urgency of work drives a "ready-fire-aim" work style. In Action Learning, groups of people consciously employ a very different approach that might be described as "ready–aim–fire–reflect–improve." This habit of reflection is central to the success of an Action Learning initiative and, for some groups and people, represents a very different way of working together.

A second transformational goal involves changes in authority and empowerment. Action Learning brings together the people who are most familiar or most keenly interested in a problem and places the power to make decisions in their hands. This can be a truly fundamental change. In many organizations, the person closest to the problem (who is often the person with the best notion about solutions) doesn't have the time, resources, or authority to implement that solution. Properly implemented, Action Learning enables team members to experience more influence in addressing thorny organizational problems. In some ways, the learning from Action Learning hinges on this one key change—placing the power to act in the hands of the people who are most intimate with the problem. (You will see this idea further explored in Chapter 6.) This change requires robust leadership support, courage, and true commitment to empowerment.

Successful Action Learning requires recognition, support, and buy-in from all interested parties. Eric at GPI faces these challenges and more as he works to get started with Action Learning.

Launching Action Learning at GPI

Eric and John Bryant, a Vice President of Product Development at GPI, were discussing the purpose of Action Learning. "I'm happy to be a Business Issue Sponsor and lend my name to your efforts if it will help you make progress, Eric, but I'm quite busy. What will I need to do?" John asked.

Eric explained, "As a sponsor, you have an opportunity to help shape the focus of the team. The team will be working on issues that run across many business units. We want them to check in with you periodically, especially when they run into roadblocks. We don't expect you to have answers for them. Instead, we want you to be a sounding board, ensure that they are working on the right issue, and redirect them if they get off track."

"As long as the team works on a project connected to product innovation or customer satisfaction, it will be a good use of my time. Why don't I just give them a project from my action list? I could always use a few more hands," said John.

Eric thought for a minute. "This could be tricky. I want John's involvement and support but I can't let him turn this into a task force for his own projects. I'd better address this head-on before his expectations get out of control."

Eric began, "Actually John, the teams might work on projects similar to those you mentioned. We have a specific process for selecting projects. First we invite a group of sponsors, such as you and your colleagues, to help identify critical challenges that cut across businesses, such as customer satisfaction and product innovation. We meet with the teams and describe what makes these issues so challenging and important for GPI. Then we ask each team to choose the topic based on what generates enthusiasm in their group. Because the topics were first selected by you and your colleagues, all of them are relevant to the business. Then we'll match you with the team that chose the topic that you're most interested in."

"OK, that's reasonable," agreed John. "But what if no one selects my topics?"

"At the sponsors' orientation we will make sure that people agree that the set of topics are relevant to the business as a whole. As a senior executive in GPI, John, I hope you could still support a team working on a significant business issue, even if it weren't directly related to your functional area," urged Eric.

"Of course," John nodded. "Besides, you never know — I may need to recruit some of these high potentials in a year or two."

As Eric left the meeting, he felt that he had John's support, but realized that he needed to be much more explicit on how the Action Learning process would be set up. As Program Manager, he needed to clarify how they would choose topics and what he needed from sponsors. "John's a great guy," Eric reflected. "But I should have known he would naturally gravitate toward projects that advance his own agenda. If I view this as an Organization Development initiative, not just a learning project, I've got to anticipate that every stakeholder will want to know 'what's in it for me.' My job is to clarify expectations and really shape how they join the process."

How to Launch Action Learning

*A*ction Learning in your organization needs support, sustainable momentum, and a trajectory for success. The best chance for long-term support beyond one cycle of Action Learning comes from involving stakeholders in designing the process for your organization.

- Momentum is needed to overcome anticipated resistance, even the resistance generated by the initiative itself.

- An Action Learning trajectory or course is established by the goals set early in the design phase and through the empowerment of the Action Learning teams to take action. Improve trajectory by fighting the tendency either to select "make work" projects or pure task force projects.

To set the most optimal course, establish goals with real outcomes so the resulting action will have a better chance to reach its potential for impact. The impact of one successful Action Learning initiative will support future Action Learning.

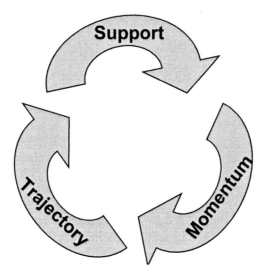

Like any organizational change, the key lies with the initial involvement of stakeholders in designing the process of Action Learning that best fits an organization.

In this section, we will explore three important questions that must be answered to ensure Action Learning success:
- How do you identify appropriate projects for Action Learning?
- Who should be involved?
- What's needed in terms of preparation and communication?

How to Identify the Appropriate Projects for Action Learning

The Action Learning Program Manager works with Business Issue Sponsors to define appropriate projects for Action Learning. The sponsor (or group of sponsors) surfaces a set of key challenges and invites Action Learning teams to select from these issues. This partnership ensures that the projects already have senior-level support and teams work on issues that are relevant to senior executives.

The Process for Defining a Business Issue

Project selection and scope are critically important.

- If project topics are not vitally important to participants, complex enough to require reflective attention and critical thinking, or within the sphere of influence of group members, they will fail.
- If the projects are appropriate, there will be high motivation to make a difference, openness to new ideas in the Action Learning format, and new outcomes otherwise unavailable to the organization.

There are several options for identifying Action Learning projects. All of these generation/selection approaches ensure that the selected project will be relevant to Business Issue Sponsors and Executive Panel members and generate personal commitment from the learning team.

Top-down Approach. Work with organizational leaders to identify issues and problems, and link the Action Learning teams to the issue.

1. Work with senior leaders to generate a list of topics where they see opportunity for Action Learning to make a difference through new ideas, new approaches, and critical analysis. Once a list is established, work with the leadership team to prioritize the topics.

2. Identify an issue from the prioritized topic areas and a Business Issue Sponsor. This sponsor will work most closely with the team. The rest of the leadership team will assume the role of the Executive Panel.
3. The Business Issue Sponsor will work with the Program Manager or an external Action Learning consultant to provide input into the team selection and formation, identifying key talent related to the issue.
4. At the launch, the sponsor will brief the Action Learning team.

Issue-driven Approach. In this approach, Program Managers or Action Learning consultants identify issues first, and then find Sponsors and teams.
1. The Program Manager or Action Learning consultant identifies potential issues. In some cases, the strategy department or the senior leadership of the organization has a list of key initiatives that need to be addressed. Executives, participant's managers, and participants are also good sources for identifying issues.
2. The Program Manager recruits Action Learning participants by giving them the chance to opt in on an issue.
3. The Program Manager charges the newly formed team with the task of recruiting sponsors.

Team-generated Approach. Identified groups of learners generate their own Action Learning projects, and then recruit sponsors.
1. Action Learning teams receive guidelines for selecting issues.
2. A team selects one of the issues or, in some instances, the team members decide to support each other for individual Action Learning initiatives.
3. The team identifies and gains support from sponsors.

Worksheets

The following worksheets can be used with any of these approaches to help identify issues. The worksheets may seem similar, but each has a slightly different set of questions. The Project Manager should choose the one(s) that works best.

Identify Issues through Brainstorming

Bring together potential sponsors or team members. Describe the criterion for Action Learning projects, and then engage in this brainstorming activity:

1. Post flip chart papers around the room, one for each participant.

2. Ask participants to record their proposed issue on the flip charts.

3. Have participants silently move around the room and view the issues, recording comments and questions as they see fit.

4. Address each issue in a random pattern. Seek to understand and make clear each issue's importance and potential impact.

Define a Business Issue

1. Name and describe the business issue.

2. Why is this issue important to your organization?

3. How does this issue impact the customer?

4. Who are potential stakeholders?

5. Who could be a potential Business Issue Sponsor?

6. If addressed, how could a solution add value and provide benefit to your organization?

Identify a Business Issue

Identify a critical or important business issue or opportunity that could benefit from new or creative thinking.

- Is it significant to the business, with important consequences associated with success or failure of the project?   YES   NO
- Is it within your control or can you successfully influence the issue?   YES   NO
- Can this project or task be accomplished within a six-month time frame?   YES   NO
- Are the members of the team free to investigate the cause of the issue?   YES   NO
- Are the members of the team free to apply creative solutions?   YES   NO
- Are the members of the team free to evaluate results?   YES   NO

Evaluate Potential Issues

As you consider potential issues to tackle, answer these questions:
- Is this a recurring issue?
- Does this issue truly need to be resolved?
- Does the issue reach beyond one business unit or function?
- Is a new level of performance needed?

If you answered yes to any of the above questions:
- What has been done to address the issue so far?
- Why take an Action Learning approach rather than another approach?

Write a Narrative Account

Ask each potential sponsor to write a narrative account, using the questions below. If helpful, use a time line to describe events relating to the issue.

As the sponsor writes his or her case, the following should be included:

1. When did he or she first notice the problem, opportunity, or issue?
2. What is the impact of this problem, opportunity, or issue?
3. What would happen if no action were taken to address the issue?
4. What are the costs to the organization in terms of individual, financial, and/or cultural impact?

One goal of Action Learning is that participants learn to access and use data more effectively. Collect reports, data, and information that were used to interpret the business issue. The data may include the following:

1. Internal reports
2. External reports
3. Brief descriptions of important conversations about the issue

Identify leadership, management, and technical skills important to addressing this issue. What are the most important skills that leaders will need in this situation?

Ask the sponsor to prepare a brief (20 minutes) presentation. Ask him or her to describe the issue and make a case for addressing it. The sponsor should be prepared to present the case and answer questions.

Define a Business Problem

Define the Problem.

- What business problem do you propose for an Action Learning team?
- Who should be involved in addressing this issue?
- Who is most knowledgeable about this issue?
- What solutions have been tried before?
- Why is this issue important? (Probe further here)
- What level of the organization does it impact? Customers? Processes? Systems?

Evaluate Success.

- How will you define success?
- Do metrics already exist?
- When can or should this outcome be measured? Before, during, or after the project?
- Will results be compared to another cycle, standard, or norm?

Support Action Learning.

If you propose a project, will you support Action Learning team efforts in the following ways:
- Attend key meetings with Action Learning teams?
- Supply resources?
- Review recommendations seriously?
- Take action on appropriate recommendations?

Guidelines for Action Learning Projects

- *Choose a real problem that's important. "Make work" poisons the Action Learning process in ways that may not be recoverable. The problem must be a real organizational problem, task, or issue that exists in a real time frame. Executive Sponsors should foresee some important consequences associated with the success or failure of the project.*

- *Choose a problem, not a puzzle. Real problems have many possible good (or tolerable) answers, not a single correct solution (Marquardt 1999).*

- *Make the problem challenging, not overwhelming. The project must be feasible; that is, it must be within the competence of the group to understand the problem and identify possible solutions. The problem should also represent a stretch issue for participants. Either the problem should be within the group's sphere of responsibility or the group must be given authority to do something about the problem.*

- *Choose a problem that affects a broad part of the organization. Make sure the issue affects each person on the Action Learning team, so they see and experience the problem differently. For example, a member from Finance will have a different view than a member from Manufacturing. This range of views will help the team develop better ideas.*

- *Relate the problem to the participant's learning objectives. Also tie it to the organization's goals and program goals.*

- *Select a problem or task that participants care about and if solved, will make a difference. Action Learning groups should have the expectation and responsibility to implement their ideas and recommendations.*

Who Should Be Involved?

In any Action Learning process there are at least five important primary players: Program Manager, Executive Panel members, Business Issue Sponsors, Learning Coaches, and Team Members. Other Action Learning stakeholders who may play a role include Team Member's managers, employees, and subject matter experts. In this section we will describe the expectations for each role during each phase of the Action Learning Execution Model shown on page 25.

Program Manager

Understanding the importance of organizational support and readiness, Program Managers work closely with Executive Panel members, Business Issue Sponsors, and Learning Coaches to foster Action Learning success. Serving as a central point of contact throughout the entire execution cycle, Program Managers have unique responsibilities during each phase.

Phase 1:   Gain support, and provide briefing and educational materials to Executive Panel Members and Business Issues Sponsors. Aid sponsors in identifying appropriate business issues and, most importantly, measures of success.

Phase 2:   Work with Business Issue Sponsors to identify teams, recruit Learning Coaches, and work with them to prepare for the launch.

Phase 3:   Support Learning Coaches. Where multiple teams are in action, foster cross-team collaboration among Learning Coaches.

Phase 4:   Support Learning Coaches. Where multiple teams are in action, continue to foster cross-team collaboration between Learning Coaches. Prepare for the presentation event.

Phase 5:   Attend presentations. Follow up Action Learning with evaluation. Improve the process and initiate new teams.

Executive Panel Members

Executive Panel members play an extremely important role in Action Learning. Beginning with issue identification, Executive Panel members challenge the team with the goal and demonstrate the importance of the task to the organization through their involvement.

Phase 1: Identify appropriate business issues. Provide Program Manager with resources and access.

Phase 2: Identify Business Issue Sponsors.

Phase 3: Participate in Action Learning launch. Periodically connect with Action Learning teams, Learning Coaches, and Business Issue Sponsors. (This continues into Phase 4.)

Phase 5: Attend presentations. Make a decision and provide for implementation.

> *Watch out for the following behaviors—they will undermine an Action Learning team.*
> - *Send the message that the project is not important.*
> - *Make decisions for the team.*
> - *Defer decision making when presented with solutions.*

Business Issue Sponsors

During Action Learning, the sponsor expects innovation from the team, encourages frank dialogue and questioning, and evaluates (but does not prescribe) potential solutions. As the tasks of the Action Learning team come to a conclusion, the sponsor keeps the focus on learning and performance by holding the team accountable for both.

Sponsors can maximize the benefits of their interaction.

- Show the way — act as a role model for Action Learning.
- Support innovative thinking.
- Follow through on the best recommendations.
- Share knowledge.
- Remain engaged.
- Allow the team to productively flounder. Uncertainty engages the mind.
- Challenge the team to go beyond its initial recommendations and plans.
- Accept some degree of risk.
- Express support and enthusiasm.
- Provide clear reasons when they say "no."
- Champion their team's ideas to their peers.

Phase 2: Choose or recommend members for the team. Find people who have the ability to impact the business issue and the availability to commit to the project for the full term. The length of the project will depend on scope, complexity, available resources, and other factors. Select team members who represent varied viewpoints and backgrounds. Consider high-potential leaders who have a demonstrated ability to impact business results.

Phase 3: At launch, explore the issue with the team. Why is the issue important? What solutions have been tried before? How will success be measured? What are the team's deliverables during and following Action Learning?

Phase 4: Provide feedback. Actively support the team throughout their entire process.
- Sign off on their topic/issue.
- Guide their thinking, as requested and as appropriate.
- Secure resources, access, etc., as necessary.
- Be available as a thought partner and valued advisor.
- Hold the team accountable for their process and result.
- Evaluate the team's results and performance.

Phase 5: Take action on the recommendations, utilize the work the team has accomplished, or determine additional work that needs to be done.
- Evaluate the team's proposal for moving the issue forward.
- Make a decision on whether or not to implement the team's proposal.
- Strategize with the team on next steps.
- Challenge groups to move beyond their recommendations.
- Accept some degree of risk.
- Express enthusiasm for recommendations and recognize employees.
- Involve other managers impacted by the recommendations in the acceptance, rejection, and modification of the proposal.
- Provide clear reasons for your support or your rationale for saying no.

Team Members

Action Learning teams are deliberately diverse. To get a range of ideas, fresh approaches, and new thinking, you need people who are willing to set aside "the way we always do it." Different levels of experience, business backgrounds, and cultures all add to the richness of ideas, which leads to better solutions. The Action Learning teams come into play at Phase 3.

Phase 3:

- Complete a performance contract with fellow team members.
- Identify the team's operating norms.
- Contract with the Learning Coach and determine next steps to get started.
- Clarify the issue and gain alignment among the team members.
- Identify assumptions about the problem.
- Set the scope of the project and the team deliverables.
- Define team roles and responsibilities.
- Outline a project plan with phases, owners, and a time line.

Phase 4:

- Investigate, gather, and analyze data.
- Identify internal and external sources of information.
- Agree on the root cause and all dependent variables.
- Brainstorm to generate ideas/solutions.
- Review ideas and approaches.
- Identify the top three solutions and agree on the most feasible solution.
- Choose the preferred option.
- Formulate recommendations.
- Prepare the presentation for the Executive Panel members.
- Reflect on the team process and learning objectives.

Phase 5:

> • Present findings and recommendations to the Executive Panel members.
> • Share the work that was accomplished, the project results, and key learnings.
> • Listen to feedback.
> • Following the presentation, reflect on the sponsor's feedback.
> • Discuss any action items or next steps the team agreed to take.
> • Reflect on individual and team learning.

Learning Coaches

Beginning in Phase 3, Learning Coaches are a critical factor in the success of any Action Learning intervention. In addition to observing, evaluating, and giving feedback on the team's performance, they often have opportunities to provide one-on-one coaching.

Phase 3:

> • Contract with the team on how they will work together.
> • Observe team dynamics and team processes, and provide feedback.
> • Help team members learn how to provide peer-to-peer feedback.
> • Encourage frequent reflection on the team process and team learning.
> • Serve as a sounding board.
> • Guide the team toward achieving results.

Phase 4:

> • Show the way. Be a role model for Action Learning.
> • Support innovative thinking.
> • Follow through on best recommendations.
> • Share knowledge.
> • Remain engaged.

- Allow the team to productively flounder. Uncertainty engages the mind.
- Challenge the team to go beyond its initial recommendations and plans.
- Accept some degree of risk.
- Express support and enthusiasm.
- Provide support as needed.

Phase 5:

- Prior to the presentation, evaluate the team's proposal for moving the issue forward.
- Challenge the group to move beyond its recommendations.
- Express enthusiasm for recommendations and recognize employees.
- Provide clear reasons for support or a rationale for saying no.
- Strategize with the team on next steps.

What's Needed in Terms of Preparation and Communication?

Each stakeholder group has differing needs in terms of preparation and communication. The Program Manager has the responsibility of making sure each group is prepared.

Business Issue Sponsors	Learning Coaches
Sponsors typically want to know "How involved will I need to be?" They have multiple detailed questions, including, "Am I expected to attend all meetings?" Some sponsors will want advice on how to coach the team. Provide an orientation to sponsors. Give them a chance to network with other sponsors, and learn about the process of Action Learning and their role in it.	Most Learning Coaches want to know as much as they can about the team, the organization, and explicit goals and objectives. If multiple Action Learning projects occur simultaneously, Learning Coaches will want to know about the experiences of the other teams. Multiple projects present both an opportunity and a challenge. Successful interventions depend on the degree of collaboration among Learning Coaches.
Team Members	**Executive Panel Members**
Prior to Action Learning, potential team members will be curious about the time commitment, the process for project completion, the project, the identity of other team members, budget, workload management, and other issues. Provide an in-person orientation session and an opportunity for team members to contract with one another about project activities and time lines.	Executive Panel members are the ultimate decision makers in Action Learning. Sponsors and Executive Panel members receive very similar briefings. Executive Panel members are generally the stakeholders who set expectations for outcomes.

Conclusion

In this chapter we explored three important questions that must be answered to ensure Action Learning success:

- How do I identify appropriate projects for Action Learning?
- Who should be involved?
- What's needed in terms of preparation and communication?

Guidelines, models, and tools were presented for each of the key questions. In Chapter 4, we'll address the role of the Learning Coach in Action Learning.

4

How Do Learning Coaches Make a Difference?

Action Learning Coaching Is Not Team Facilitation

*L*earning Coaches are more than skilled facilitators and coaches. Their primary goal is to maximize and help others retain the learning that occurs at the individual, team, and organizational level. This goal requires a different approach to team facilitation and coaching. Consider the story of Joanne and Alex.

Joanne has a strong reputation within GPI as a skilled and effective task and leadership team facilitator and coach. GPI frequently asks her to facilitate task forces and retreats. When the organization decided to use Action Learning as part of its advanced leadership program, Joanne was one of the first to be nominated as a coach.

During the first Action Learning meeting, the team went through the predictable stages of team development. When the team felt stymied and frustrated, Joanne knew how to overcome obstacles, resolve problems, and keep the team moving toward a successful conclusion. She helped the team reach consensus on the charter for the project. When two strong-willed members clashed, she mediated a resolution. With her assistance, the team

49

made effective decisions. Her warm manner drew out quiet team members, and engaged even those who typically sat back and watched.

Through her facilitation efforts, the team finished on time and Joanne felt good about the final proposal. She was confident that she had served as a good role model for team leadership. However, she was less certain about what the team members had learned.

Alex is also an accomplished team leader and facilitator at another organization. He gets the most out of teams and frequently facilitates leadership team strategic planning retreats. Alex has also accepted the challenge to be a coach for his organization's advanced leadership development program. He recognizes that Action Learning will be different from the facilitation he has done in the past.

Alex attends an orientation by an outside consultant who has conducted Action Learning programs for several years and understands how to prepare experienced task facilitators and coaches for the role that is described as "Learning Coach." During a two-day training program, he not only learns the theory, he also gets an opportunity to practice Action Learning skills and receive feedback.

During the training, Alex learns that he will not take a direct and active role in guiding action during the sessions. Instead, he will ask great questions that encourage team members to reflect on what the group does to facilitate goal accomplishment and what it does to inhibit progress and prevent it from reaching its goal.

In the first meeting, Alex's team is disorganized and can't agree on the project goal. Frustrated and impatient, the team follows the direction set by its most dominant and vocal member. Alex, also frustrated, has to bite his tongue to keep from offering advice or making an observation to push the team into more productive activities. Instead, he asks a provocative question that interrupts the ineffective team discussion, and gets team members to reflect on what they are doing and how they could improve their process. "Does the team agree on the goals and objectives of this project?" With looks of chagrin and relief, people on the team admit that they don't. They begin to discuss which process changes would help them develop a more defined goal. Later, they discuss what is working well in the process and what needs improvement.

Alex's simple question dramatically improved the team process. More importantly, through its own efforts, the team learned process steps for suspending its natural bias toward action long enough to agree on goals and harness the talents and energy of all its team members.

Let's look at the experiences of Joanne and Alex:

- Joanne and Alex both got good results in terms of the end product. But Alex was more effective at facilitating learning.
- Joanne hoped that the team learned important lessons through her active facilitation. Alex was quite sure that his team learned and internalized important lessons, even if inelegantly and imperfectly formed, because they did it themselves.
- Alex made sure that these lessons were captured and retained by asking the team to identify the important lessons learned. What worked? What didn't work? What could be improved?

Michael Marquardt (2005a) has summarized the differences between being an effective Team Facilitator and a Learning Coach.

Team Facilitator	Learning Coach
Focus on group process and norms	Focus on learning and team performance
Make statements based on expertise	Ask reflective questions
Focus on what has happened	Focus on why and how, and action–consequence linkages
Foster group dependence	Foster group independence
Employ single-loop learning: • Cybernetic; i.e., actual versus desired learning • Cause and effect	Emphasize double-loop learning: • Cultivate skills of learning • Connect learning to larger business goals
Focus on the present and past	Focus on the future
Offer answers and suggest behavior	Trust that the group has better answers and insights
Generate dependent thinking	Foster self-confidence and critical thinking
Generate reaction	Generate reflection
Added value is group-dynamics expertise and cleverness	Added value is generating individual perspectives and encouraging wisdom
People and the group grow in the manner desired by the facilitator	People grow into the future they need and desire

Are You Fostering a Dependent Relationship with Your Team?

A major advantage of serving as a Learning Coach is that your team learns how to operate independently from you. Team members internalize the learning that occurs during the Action Learning project and take that learning back to their regular jobs.

However, sometimes a team can come to depend too much on a Learning Coach. Watch for the following tip-offs that this is occurring with your team or other teams:

- *The team makes jokes or refers nervously to you or other Learning Coaches. "If we get stuck, Joanne will fix it."*
- *Team members look to you for reinforcement, or to intervene any time they have a disagreement or seem unable to move forward.*
- *Team members are reluctant to take useful team leadership roles.*
- *The team wants you to be in charge of the flip chart, record ideas, manage time boundaries, and create the agenda.*
- *The team directs its frustration at you and blames you when it doesn't make progress.*

When you become aware of these indicators, clarify your role and emphasize the importance of action, reflection, and team theory-building to the goals of personal, team, and organizational learning.

Learning Coaches at GPI

Eric felt more confident about his Action Learning plan. Once he started to think about Action Learning as a broader OD intervention, pieces quickly fell into place. He was better able to clarify stakeholder roles, project guidelines, and the process by which sponsors would jointly set the stage for a range of projects.

Eric was meeting Susan Lund and Karen Chen for lunch. Eric was glad they were on board as coaches. Both had backgrounds in coaching and organization development; in Eric's view, they were real professionals.

Eric was curious about how they planned to coach their Action Learning teams. "Will you do some common start-up exercises with your teams when they meet?" asked Eric.

"Actually, no," Susan replied. "We will explain our role and help clarify the task, but we won't lead the group. Our main focus will be helping team members learn how to work together."

Eric seemed surprised. "Susan, I've seen you facilitate an executive retreat. You're fabulous at that. And Karen, last summer you guided the process improvement teams through every step of their decision process. Isn't this just a variation on what you do all the time?"

Karen explained, "This is a different type of role for a coach to play. Last summer, the business process improvement teams were set up to work on a specific agenda. It's great that participants learned something about organizational change during the process, but that wasn't the purpose. In Action Learning we not only want to work on the problem, we want people to learn how problems get solved. Most groups would be more than happy to let Susan or I take over and do all the facilitation for them, but that won't help them reflect on how they actually get work done."

Susan added, "Our job is to help them get better at being an effective team. To do that, they need to understand how they work on the problem and how they work together. Even though I find this work fun, it can be really hard because I have to be much more patient when the team is struggling. If I save them, they won't learn how to save themselves."

"Does it really matter who saves whom, as long as the team is making progress?" asked Eric.

"Absolutely," Susan asserted. "It even matters on issues as simple as choosing whether or not to manage the flip chart. I want the team to take ownership for how they define the issues and how they capture their ideas. I want them to figure out how to work through those moments when they can't make a decision. Often a group will look to the person at the flip chart to tell them what to do, especially if that person is the facilitator. In an Action Learning context, I ask the team to describe how they manage their ideas, how they make decisions, and what they do when they can't make a decision. That is part of what they learn from their work together."

Eric ventured, "If they learn these skills here, then I guess they'll be able to apply them to other projects and with other teams." Susan and Karen nodded.

Eric thought about this as they ate. "It's funny," he mused. "When we call you a coach, we assume that you will tell the team what to do."

Karen replied, "Some people think a coach adds value by giving advice or telling people what they did wrong. We think a coach is someone who asks great questions. Not just good questions, great questions! I don't just want a reaction from members of the team, I want genuine reflection on how they work together. I want them to understand how they think together and discover ways to be effective as a problem-solving group. In other words, I want to be a Learning Coach."

"When we do our job well, we see changes in the way the group thinks together," Susan continued. "Instead of quickly judging each others' ideas, they explore the assumptions behind the ideas. Instead of laying out ideas without explanation, they begin to surface their assumptions and the questions that led to their ideas. This doesn't happen right away, but you can feel the difference in a group that works this way!"

Eric sipped his drink. "I'm glad I've got you two as Learning Coaches. I'm not sure I would have your patience!"

Role of the Learning Coach

*A*ction Learning teams meet a number of times over several months to review progress, challenge each others' thinking, collect and recognize learning, engage in dialogue, and adapt their problem-solving approach to the realities they encounter as they investigate a problem in new ways.•

When you serve as a Learning Coach, you continually challenge the team's thinking and lead them toward self-facilitation.

You play a crucial role in the success of an Action Learning team. In addition to observing, evaluating, and formulating great questions that encourage the team to reflect upon its performance, you often have opportunities to provide one-on-one coaching.

As a Learning Coach, you also have these responsibilities:
- Contract with the team on how you will work with them.
- Observe team dynamics and the team process. Ask questions that encourage the team to reflect upon its behavior with the aim of improving its performance.
- Assure that Action Learning norms and principles are followed.
- Create an environment that fosters reflection and learning.

- Manage time boundaries so the team has sufficient time to summarize lessons learned.
- Serve as a sounding board on issues that arise.
- Paraphrase by using questions; e.g., "I hear you saying," "Is this what you mean?"
- Be an active liaison with sponsors.
  - Ask questions to ensure that the team maintains active ties with sponsors.
  - Periodically meet with sponsors to keep them informed and involved in the project.

Assess Your Skills as a Learning Coach

Even though you may be an experienced and confident team facilitator, there may be gaps in your current skill set as a Learning Coach. Answer the following questions:

- *How is an Action Learning team different from other teams you have facilitated?*
- *What skills do you need to add, retain, or let go of to address these differences?*
- *Think of facilitator behaviors that were successful with other types of teams. Would any of those behaviors be less appropriate for an Action Learning team?*
- *What will you need to remember as you adapt your facilitation approach to Action Learning teams?*

Adapted from Freedman, 1998

The Basic Rule for Action Learning Coaches

Complex and significant personal, team, and organizational learning, a primary goal of Action Learning, occurs only as a result of reflection (Bruner, 1974; Bandura, 1977; Knowles, Holton, & Swanson, 1998). It is impossible to reflect without considering a question (Marquardt, 2005).

So, the Basic Rule for Action Learning Coaches is clear: lead with questions whenever possible. Questions help you promote the essential active ingredient for effective Action Learning, which is reflective inquiry. In normal discussions, people lead with statements and judgments. Statements, particularly when they aren't agreed upon, encourage others to state their opinion and judgment on an issue. Quite naturally, people focus on the strengths of their opinions and judgments, and the gaps and inadequacies of the views of others. Assertions are met with counterarguments, which all too often result in debate and defensiveness. Leading with questions achieves a balance between advocacy and inquiry, a key requirement for dialogue (Marquardt, 2004).

Questions encourage people to reflect on the following:
- Sources of information
- Gaps in understanding or clarity
- Assumptions underlying opinions
- Contradictions
- Reasons for behavior
- Implications of statements

Effective Questions

Effective questions facilitate reflection and creative thinking. Here are some guidelines to help you promote learning and optimal team functioning.

Open-ended questions

Open-ended questions give individuals a high degree of freedom in deciding how to respond. They encourage people to elaborate on their ideas, reactions, and feelings. They also encourage people to think expansively, critically, and analytically.

To form open-ended questions, use key words: who, what, where, how, why.
- **Who.** Who has access to the information that the team needs?
- **What.** What other solutions to this kind of problem are you aware of?
- **Where.** Where else can you get information about this issue?
- **How.** How is the team going to get the support of senior management?
- **Why.** Why do you think this worked?

> *"Why" questions encourage the team to reflect on the cause and effect aspects of a situation.*
>
> *Marquardt, 2005b*

Types of open-ended questions include (adapted from Marquardt, 2005b):
- Affective: encourage sharing of feelings
- Reflective: encourage more elaboration
- Probing: challenge basic assumptions
- Creating connections: create systems perspectives
- Clarifying: improve the clarity of a message or statement
- Exploratory: open up new avenues and insights that lead to new explorations
- Analytical: examine cause and effect, not just symptoms

Closed Questions

Closed questions encourage a single answer, usually "yes" or "no." Although the use of closed questions is often discouraged in many communications courses, they do serve a purpose and have a place in a Learning Coach's repertoire. In contrast to open-ended questions, which encourage fruitful dialogue and expand the team's understanding of the issue, closed questions bring issues to an end.

Closed questions can be used to:
- Limit debate and make decisions; e.g., "Is the team ready to make a decision?"
- Find out specific information; e.g., "When is the proposal due?"
- Identify preferences; e.g., "Does the team like Plan A or Plan B?"

Unhelpful Questions

Most questions from a Learning Coach are perceived as helpful, even if they're provocative. However, some questions should be avoided.

Leading Questions

Leading questions, a staple of trial attorneys, are intended to elicit predetermined, specific answers. Because your role as a Learning Coach is to get the team to make its own decisions to the extent possible, leading questions are generally unhelpful. Guard against using this type of question when the team feels frustrated by a lack of progress in resolving key issues. For example, avoid questions like, "Can't the team see that A is the best option?"

Multiple Questions

When the team doesn't get the right point or doesn't make connections between issues, it's easy to become frustrated or impatient. You might be tempted to respond with a string of questions, some of them leading. Remember: multiple questions can make a discussion feel like an interrogation.

Judgmental Questions

David Cooperrider (1999) noted that questions have a great influence on the direction of growth and learning. If a Learning Coach's questions focus on finding fault and blame, people will learn to be defensive and make excuses for their behavior and choices rather than exploring how their learning could improve outcomes and situations. So it is imperative that your questions do not come across as judgmental.

Sometimes it will be difficult for you to ask questions without revealing your opinions. If you strongly disagree (privately, of course) with the team's decision or direction, they will detect your opinions by the form of your questions. When teams perceive criticism, they commonly feel defensive and close down. Obviously, this reaction is not conducive to learning.

Examples of questions that can be perceived as judgmental include:
• What did the team do wrong here?
• What mistakes were made regarding this issue?
• Who can help Andrew understand this point?
• Why is it taking the team so long to come up with a solution?

You could convey the same intent by emphasizing learning rather than criticism in your questions.
• How could the team improve upon its performance?
• What could the team do differently to get a better result?
• Are there other approaches to the issues that Andrew raised?
• How could the team speed up its problem-solving process?

You can make your questions more helpful by employing a learner rather than a judger mind-set (Marquardt, 2005b). Some useful distinctions are found on the next page.

Judger	Learner
Judgmental (of self and others)	Accepting (of self and others)
Reactive and automatic	Responsive and thoughtful
Know-it-already	Values ambiguity
Blame	Responsibility
Inflexible and rigid	Flexible and adaptive
Either/or thinking	Both/and thinking
Self-righteous	Inquisitive
Personal perspective only	Considers perspectives of others
Defends assumptions	Questions assumptions
More statements and assumptions	More questions and curiosity
Possibilities seen as limited	Possibilities seen as unlimited
Primary mood: protective	Primary mood: curiosity

Marquardt, 2005b, adapted from Adams, M. (2004)

Learning Coach's Toolbox

The following tools are very useful for dealing with specific stages or issues that emerge during an Action Learning project. Use them within the basic structure of Action Learning and the basic rule of leading with questions. If you apply a learner mind-set and model curiosity, reflection, and open-mindedness, you will be able to use the following tools and interventions in a flowing and seamless manner.

Tool 1: Asking Great Questions

- Keep your advice to yourself, especially during the clarifying phase. Jumping in with suggestions for quick fixes undermines the whole process. Plus, quick fixes may be the reason why this issue became a problem in the first place.
- Get everyone's input. Ask members to describe their thoughts about the problem or issue.
- Listen patiently and well. Interruptions are deadly to the dialogue process. Action Learning calls for the most careful listening you will ever do.

The Art of Finding Great Questions

People who ask great questions demonstrate imagination, creativity, systems thinking, and a great sense of timing. Peter Senge (Senge et al, 1999) offers the following advice to Learning Coaches who want to develop the ability to ask really great questions.

- *Assess the landscape. Look for the larger context, scan the horizon as well as the contours of the current organizational landscape, notice indicators that point to "storms" as well as "sunny skies."*
- *Discover core questions. Develop patterns or sequences of questions, cluster questions and consider the relationships between them, notice what emerges to uncover deeper themes.*
- *Create images of possibilities. Encourage people to use their imaginations to consider what could be if the big questions were answered, create vivid images of possibilities.*
- *Evolve workable strategies. Notice and identify workable strategies that emerge in response to compelling questions and to images of possibilities that these questions provoke.*

- Question assumptions, especially your own. Don't assume that a situation you experienced is similar to the one you're hearing about now. The greatest learning will be in the differences.
  - Ask questions.
  - What information is missing?
  - What are the unanswered questions?
  - Are there missing facts or figures?
  - Do you need to investigate and validate assumptions?
  - Do you need to seek opinions outside the group?
- Encourage reflection. Don't go along with premature action without adequate reflection. "Ready-shoot-aim" is the source of many problems. If your team leaps to a solution before you think they have considered it carefully, it's your responsibility to use questions to make sure the "thinking work" gets done.
- Question generalizations. Listen for words that mask sloppy thinking: everybody, always, never, nobody ever. When you hear a generalization, ask about the exceptions.
- Reflect on how the whole team is learning. When it comes to learning, the whole is greater than the sum of its parts. The point for team members is to develop themselves and to develop as a team, so that the whole practice of Action Learning will benefit.

Tool 2: The Typical Action Learning Problem-Solving Process

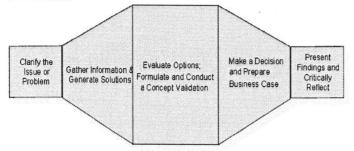

This figure presents the typical phases that a team goes through to effectively solve a difficult and complex problem. Using the right question or intervention at the right time will help team members learn for themselves which processes and activities are most effective.

Phase 1: Clarify the Issue or Problem

The goal of Phase 1 is to clarify the team's understanding of the problem or opportunity facing the organization. By the end of this phase, team members should have a clear understanding of what defines success. "What" questions are most appropriate in this phase; they promote the gathering of information as well as clarification of and agreement on the goal (Marquardt, 2005b).

Use the following questions to clarify the problem:
- What problem will this team solve?
- How does this problem or opportunity affect you?
- What's the real impact on your organization?
- What information is known? Unknown?
- What are your assumptions about the problem?
- What questions do you want to ask others outside of the group?

Sometimes the team will have difficulty owning the problem. If team members were assigned to teams, the problem may not be their top choice. Perhaps the team believes that the problem is too big or vague. Problems in ownership or commitment at early phases in the process must be addressed if the team is to move forward. Otherwise the team will make excuses to minimize the importance or feasibility of the problem, and will make a half-hearted or minimal effort to develop a creative and effective solution.

Here are examples of questions that will help the team own the problem and move forward with commitment.
- What's in it for individuals, the team, and the organization to find a solution to this problem?
- What are the consequences if the team doesn't fully commit to developing a solution to this problem?
- How can you modify the scope of the problem?

- What additional information is required to clarify the problem?
- What would it take for the team to fully accept and own this problem?
- What keeps this problem from being a top priority?

Phase 2: Gather Information and Generate Solutions

In this phase, team members gather and share information to help solve the business issue or problem. One pitfall that the team faces is the tendency to stop after they surface and share the most basic information. At this point, you can use questions to challenge the team to be more comprehensive in its data gathering. Ask the team:

- Where can you find important information?
- Who can help you solve this problem?
- Who else has this problem?
- What could this problem be related to?
- How is this problem different from other problems?
- What parts of the problem can you control or not control?
- What are the limitations? What is allowed and what is ruled out? Can the rules be changed?
- Who are the more visible stakeholders of this issue/problem?
- Who are less visible but clearly impacted stakeholders?

In this phase, "why" questions are often appropriate. Reflective, probing, analytical, and exploratory questions help you encourage the team to slow down, examine assumptions, and dig beneath the initial presenting of problems or symptoms. This helps the team develop fresh insights that change the fundamental direction of their inquiry and work.

Next, the team generates a large number of creative ideas about solutions for the problem or opportunity by using "how" questions. Again, a team's strong desire to solve problems as quickly and efficiently as possible can be an obstacle. The most creative and effective solutions are not usually generated from the quickest, most efficient processes.

Graffiti Activity: The Graffiti activity helps team members generate a large set of possible solutions for their Action Learning problem. Participants post their ideas without trying to categorize or evaluate the responses.

1. Give each person a large sheet of paper.

2. For 15 minutes, have individuals list as many ideas as possible for solving the problem.
   - Emphasize that you want quantity, not quality.
   - Ask individuals to be as creative as possible.
   - Ignore issues of feasibility, cost, and popularity, for the time being.

3. At the end of 15 minutes, post each person's list on the wall.

4. Introduce process and structure concepts without violating the Basic Rule. Ask the following questions:
   - How satisfied are you with the quality of the ideas generated? (typical response: "Not that satisfied." "We're only considering a few ideas." "People are ignoring my ideas.")
   - What can the team do to generate more ideas from more people? (typical response: "We can't think of anything else." "Nothing else would work." "People would never support that idea.")
   - Would the team be interested in learning about a process that would generate more ideas from more people? (typical response: "I guess so." "Yeah, maybe that would help.")

Although it is unlikely that the team will reject your offer, it's better to introduce idea-generation techniques in this way. This gives the team the option to say "no." Given that there are instances when you need to shift from asking questions to making statements, it is important to maintain the Basic Rule as often as possible.

Getting the Right Amount of Structure

As noted earlier, the Kolb Learning Cycle (1984) represents a useful model to guide a Learning Coach's interventions.

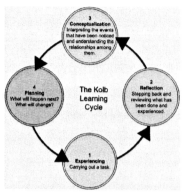

As a Learning Coach, you will primarily intervene with great questions to promote reflective observation, abstract conceptualization, and active experimentation. From time to time in the Action Learning process, the learning cycle gets blocked, usually by faulty team processes. As a skilled task facilitator, quickly diagnose the root cause of the team's derailment but fight the temptation to step in. If you remove the obstacle, you will diminish the opportunity for significant learning.

In most cases, you can show good judgment by remaining silent or by asking open-ended questions (affective, reflective, probing, connecting, clarifying, exploratory, and analytical) to facilitate the team's discovery and learning. However, if the team stumbles so badly in a process area that their project's success is in jeopardy, you need to balance the opportunity for learning with the need to produce a reasonable product. After all, Action Learning is not just an intellectual exercise to satisfy curiosity and facilitate learning. In most cases, the organization is counting on the team to produce a solid, innovative solution. Letting the team fail for the sake of learning is unacceptable.

When you must intervene more actively, follow these general guidelines:

- Ask a question that identifies the process difficulty. "Why is the team having so much difficulty coming to a decision?"
- Ask open-ended questions to promote reflection and deep thinking about the problem, and encourage active experimentation. Example: "How can you use what you learned today in other situations?"
- Encourage team members to make the decision that they will not be able to come up with a reasonable solution given the available time.
- Ask team members if they would like to learn about a process approach or technique that would help them overcome the roadblock.
- Describe the process or technique, if invited.

Limit your intervention to process recommendations and refrain from offering task solutions. If you are a line or functional manager as well as a Learning Coach, the temptation to make suggestions or recommendations regarding project solutions may be particularly strong. Before you use a more directive intervention, reflect on the consequences of providing more structure.

- Are the consequences of the team's floundering at a particular point so serious as to jeopardize the entire project?
- What learning opportunities will be sacrificed if you offer more structure at this time?

As you become more skilled and experienced as a Learning Coach, your ability to ask really great questions will reduce the need to provide additional structuring interventions.

Phase 3: Evaluate Options; Formulate and Conduct a Concept Validation

The goal of this phase is to winnow down the list of ideas to identify the best ones. Teams typically find it difficult to narrow the focus and come to a consensus. The complexity of reaching a team decision is a primary reason for the difficulty.

Narrow the Field. Teams using effective brainstorming methods, such as the Graffiti Activity, can easily generate 30 to 40 ideas. If the team is struggling to reduce this set, ask team members if they would be interested in learning a process for quickly narrowing the field to a small, more manageable number. (Again, getting to this question may require a series of questions to set up the need for you to introduce this tool.)

Then, have the team proceed as follows:
- Review and discuss each idea so that everyone understands what the ideas mean.
- Collapse and condense similar ideas so that the resulting list has as little redundancy as possible.
- Vote on the ideas. Give each team member three to five votes (the larger the team, the smaller number of votes per person) to choose the ideas they think are best, based on their own criteria.
- Determine which ideas received the most votes, and decide which ideas will go on to the next phase of more intense discussion.

Evaluate Top Ideas. The team is now ready to evaluate the top ideas. As team members discuss their selection criteria, you will likely notice differences of opinion regarding the importance of a criteria and ratings on each criteria. Good questions at this point include:
- How will the team resolve differences of opinion?
- How can the team identify common ground?
- What factors would persuade team members to change or modify their opinions about the top ideas?

- What modifications to the ideas would satisfy the top priorities of team members?
- What method and criteria will the team use to make decisions?

If your team struggles to resolve conflicts and doesn't seem able to bridge differences in opinion, it's time to introduce conflict management and consensus building strategies. Use a model for developing consensus, such as PDI's Talk-Listen model.

Phase 4: Make a Decision and Prepare a Business Case

Teams typically do not consider the range of decision-making strategies before they make important decisions. They often follow the recommendation of the most dominant team members or

---

Talk-Listen Model

Connect
Establish rapport and make a personal connection.

Frame
Establish the context and set clear expectations for your conversation.

Explore
Clarify your perspective and use listening to explore the perspectives of others.

Align
Combine the list of everyone's most important needs into one list.

Solve
Solve the problem now that you have have a clearly defined set of needs from all parties.

Execute
Set clear expectations about who will do what and when it will happen.

Follow-up
Schedule follow-up or review sessions to fine-tune your solution.

Ongoing Relationship
Keep the relationship going to make future interactions easier and more productive.

---

use simple majority decision rules to resolve all conflicts. If you observe people using these suboptimal procedures, ask the questions on the next page to prompt reflection on their decision-making process.

- What options does the team have for making decisions?
- Under what conditions would the team use each method?
- What are the predictable consequences of using the decision-making method the team selected (consciously or by default)?
- What decision-making method would be most appropriate for this decision?

In answering these questions, team members will probably note that more important questions require a higher degree of consensus. Confirm that problems with high requirements for quality (high negative consequences for a bad decision) or acceptance (high negative consequences for a lack of acceptance by stakeholders) are best decided through a more lengthy consensus-building process.

Phase 5: Present Findings and Critically Reflect

The purpose of this phase is to create an opportunity for participants to stop and reflect on the lessons of their experience. Participants focus on four key questions:

- What was our goal?
- What happened?
- What would we do differently?
- What did we learn?

Tool 3: Team Dynamics

The success of an Action Learning project is highly related to the degree to which the Action Learning team becomes a high-performance team. PDI's TeamWise® Success Model presents critical success factors.

The following questions will encourage your team to reflect on the issues identified by the TeamWise® Success Model.

TeamWise® Success Model

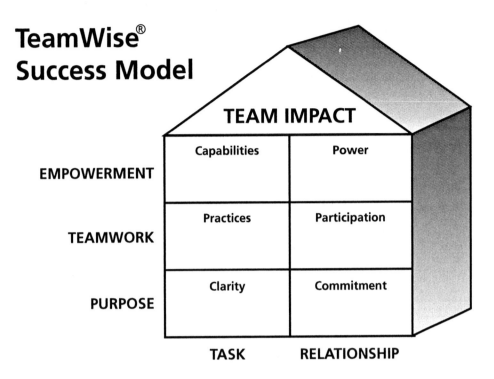

TEAM IMPACT

	Capabilities	Power
EMPOWERMENT		
TEAMWORK	Practices	Participation
PURPOSE	Clarity	Commitment

TASK   **RELATIONSHIP**

Clarity

Reflect on the degree to which the team has a clear understanding of its collective purpose and performance expectations.

- Does the team know how its goals align with the organization's goals?
- Does the team know what it is expected to produce as a team?
- Does the team know how its deliverables will be evaluated?

Commitment

Reflect on the degree to which the team believes in the importance of the work it does and how dedicated it is to high performance.

- What keeps team members from speaking about the team and its mission in an enthusiastic and positive way outside of team meetings?

- What would it take for team members to willingly sacrifice personal interests for the good of the team?
- What factors keep team members from fulfilling their commitments to this team? What can be done to remove these issues?

Practices

Reflect on the degree to which the team uses effective processes, tools, and procedures to manage its work.

- What can the team do to coordinate its work more efficiently and effectively?
- How well does the team make decisions? What can be done to improve decision making?
- How well does the team ensure that each member knows what to do and what he or she is accountable for?
- How can the team improve its ability to execute its plans?
- How well does the team manage meetings to make the most effective use of time? How could it do a better job managing its time?

Participation

Reflect on the degree to which the team develops collaborative relationships to ensure full involvement and contribution.

- How can team members improve the degree of trust they have for each other?
- How well does the team work through difficult issues until they are resolved? What can be done to improve in this area?
- How can the team improve the way it values the diverse perspectives of individuals on the team?
- What can be done to increase the willingness of team members to invest time and resources to develop the team's skills and capabilities?

- How can the team get the right mix of knowledge, skills, and experience to achieve its goals?
- What can be done to gain access to resources that the team needs to achieve its goals?

Capabilities

Reflect on the degree to which the team has the capability to achieve its objectives.
- How well is the team achieving its objectives?
- Are the team members producing better results by working together than by working separately? What can be done to improve the value of working together?
- What could the team do to ensure that it is developing and improving as a team?

Power

Reflect on the degree to which the team has the collective will and confidence it needs to succeed despite obstacles.
- How much freedom does the team have to take the actions it considers necessary? What can be done to improve its power?
- What can be done to increase the team's confidence in its ability to achieve its goals?
- What can the team do to ensure that its decisions are supported by the organization's leadership?

Tool 4: Midterm Team Performance Questionnaire

Midway through the Action Learning project, ask team members to formally assess the team's performance. As the Learning Coach, make sure that the team takes the lead in analyzing the questionnaire results.

The team may try to avoid filling out the questionnaire, especially if they're not making satisfactory progress. In that case, use a series of questions to prompt action:

- Has the team analyzed the results of the Midterm Team Performance Questionnaire?
- (If the team has not analyzed results) Why do you think the team collected the data but hasn't analyzed it yet?
- (If the team has not filled out the questionnaire) What can the team learn from the results of the questionnaire?

Take care not to scold or judge your group. If you maintain an attitude of curiosity, you can help the team be less defensive about completing the questionnaire and help them reflect on why their team (or any team) avoids self-evaluation.

This questionnaire will help you and your team members honestly assess the performance of your Action Learning team. While the responses may be collected and compared across teams, the primary purpose of this assessment is to provide data back to your team on its performance. This will give you and your team an understanding of what *you as a team* believe is necessary to improve performance.

Give the team the following instructions: Think about the team, how it works together, and the results it produces as you answer the questions on the survey.

Scale:
5 = To a Very Great Extent
4 = To a Great Extent
3 = To Some Extent

2 = To a Little Extent
1 = Not at All

	Not at All	Little	Some	Great	Very Great
We trust each other.	1	2	3	4	5
We value the diverse perspectives of individuals on this team.	1	2	3	4	5
We know how our team's goals align with the organization's goals.	1	2	3	4	5
Overall, this team produces better results by working together than individuals would achieve by working separately.	1	2	3	4	5
We have access to the resources we need to achieve our goals.	1	2	3	4	5
Team members fulfill their commitments to the team.	1	2	3	4	5
Team members are willing to sacrifice personal interests for the good of the team.	1	2	3	4	5
Our team has the right mix of knowledge, skills, and experience to achieve our goals.	1	2	3	4	5
Team members effectively coordinate their work to achieve team goals.	1	2	3	4	5
We feel we are free to take the actions we think are necessary.	1	2	3	4	5
We surface and work through difficult issues until they are resolved.	1	2	3	4	5
Our leaders support our team's decisions.	1	2	3	4	5
We know how to make decisions as a team.	1	2	3	4	5
We know that we are expected to produce as a team.	1	2	3	4	5
Our team is confident that we can achieve our goals.	1	2	3	4	5

	Not at All	Little	Some	Great	Very Great
We make sure we are always developing and improving as a team.	1	2	3	4	5
We invest time and resources to develop our team's skills and capabilities.	1	2	3	4	5
Team members speak and act in a unified way, both during and outside of team meetings.	1	2	3	4	5
We plan and manage meetings to make effective use of time.	1	2	3	4	5
We achieve our objectives.	1	2	3	4	5
We establish specific action steps and assign accountabilities to ensure our goals are achieved.	1	2	3	4	5
We know how our team's performance will be measured.	1	2	3	4	5

Comments for Improvement

What additional resources are needed?

What information does the team still need?

What are your suggestions for improving the performance of your Action Learning team?

5
What Actually Happens?

In Chapter 4, we explored the role of the Learning Coach. In this chapter, we're going to focus on each phase of the Action Learning process, providing guidelines and useful tools. Reflecting on the need to capture and use the knowledge generated from day-to-day experience, Edward Deming said, "Learning is not compulsory … neither is survival."

The original parameters of what we now know as Action Learning were explored in the problem-solving practices of managers in the British coal mines of the 1940s. "Soon after World War II, in Britain, Geoffrey Vickers, Director of the Manpower Department of the National Coal Board, set up groups of managers from the coal pits to study conditions in the mines. Reg Revans, then Director of Education for the mines, suggested small group discussions. These manager groups found communication issues, some of which arose from their own practices. They instituted changes which resulted in drastically fewer accidents. Reg Revans and Gaston Deurinck - from Belgium's Industrie Universite, concluded that learning is a social process, that people learn best from other people in the same situation; managers learn best from other managers. Referred to as peer learning, its success lies in the mutual identification of interests or problems and the social restraint on authoritarianism among equals" (McNulty, 1979).

The one constant of Action Learning, whether in organizations or educational institutions, has been the Action Learning team (or Action Learning set).

Teams engaged in Action Learning typically meet over several months to review progress, challenge each others' thinking, collect and recognize learning, engage in dialogue, and adapt their problem-solving approach to the realities they encounter as they investigate the problem in new ways. The members of an Action Learning team provide each other with a meaningful, action-oriented relationship that often extends beyond the term of the formal team process.

Characteristics that Lead to an Action Learning Team's Success

Norms, the "rules" of how to work together on a team, often include confidentiality, respect, fair sharing of time, and focused listening. Teams develop norms as they work together.

Team Norms

Teams often set norms in the following areas:
- Scheduling, including who has the authority to place meetings on calendars
- Frequency of face-to-face meetings and teleconferences
- Attendance requirements
- Expectations on how quickly team members should respond to voice mail and e-mail, and protocols for using "Reply" or "Reply to All"
- How and when to develop and distribute agendas for team meetings
- How to record and distribute minutes and action items (timing and methods)
- Who will facilitate meetings
- How to accomplish major work; project planning

- How and where to store information and documents (e.g., intranet site, shared files)
- Who will be the point of contact with the sponsor
- Who will communicate with stakeholders outside the team
- How to make decisions
- How to handle conflict
- How to maintain energy and commitment to the project

Accountability

Since Action Learning focuses on actual, tough work projects, it's expected that team members will do what they say and honestly report what happened so the information can be useful in the next session.

Interdependence

This is real work, and showing up and paying attention is a necessary part of working with an Action Learning team. When team members talk about their project, they depend on others to push the right questions and help people see what they might otherwise miss.

Group Size

The optimal group size is six to eight members.

Group Diversity

Action Learning teams should be diverse. Diversity of ideas, fresh approaches, and new thinking all depend on people who are willing to set aside "the way we always do it." A range of experience levels, business backgrounds, and cultures add to the richness of ideas, which leads to better solutions.

Learning Coach

As discussed in Chapter 4, the Learning Coach is a critical element of successful Action Learning. The Learning Coach intervenes lightly and generally, using questions to help the group make progress and learn.

Team Leadership

Leadership on an Action Learning team tends to emerge and shift. The very best Action Learning teams successfully generate a form of collaborative leadership.

Shared Learning Process

In successful Action Learning, critical reflection becomes a habit that team members insist upon.

Ownership of Goals

Even in situations where problem statements are given to the group, a high-performing Action Learning team will reframe the problem, restating it to encourage ownership and buy-in by the team members.

Conflict Resolution Goals

Action Learning can be an intense experience, particularly when there is a high level of visibility and accountability. Therefore, conflict resolution is a critical competency for Action Learning teams.

An agreed-upon process for conflict resolution is characteristic of a high-performing Action Learning team.

GPI: Action Learning in Action

Several months after the launch of Action Learning, the GPI teams were engaged and active. Meetings occurred regularly and Eric sensed a positive buzz about Action Learning.

One afternoon, James Burg, Senior Vice President of HR, stopped by Eric's office. "Hi Eric. I just saw John Bryant, one of your sponsors. He certainly seems pleased with the overall progress of Action Learning. His team is coming up with some interesting ideas!"

"I'm glad he is finding it valuable," replied Eric. "So are the team members."

"Good," smiled James. "Then you won't mind preparing an interim summary for our executive committee meeting next month. Nothing elaborate. Just some overall trends and data on progress to date."

After James left, Eric became uneasy. Although he got general updates from the Learning Coaches and a few team members, he didn't have anything structured. He wondered if he should have set up a formal evaluation measure at the beginning of the Action Learning process. What should he measure? If a team were making progress on the task but not learning anything in the process, were they performing better than a team making slow progress but learning how to analyze and reshape a problem together?

Now Eric was concerned. What should he report to the executive committee? How did the teams and Learning Coaches know they were making progress?

He knew that he wanted a positive message. Eric resolved to get a better sense of what was happening in the Action Learning teams.

Launching Action Learning

*A*ction Learning success requires role and purpose clarity, teamwork, and critical reflection skills. Three important events occur during the launch: problem introduction, team formation, and orientation. By the end of launch, participants should have a clear picture of success, both from a learning and organizational results perspective.

Launch Day Agenda

20 minutes   The Program Manager introduces Action Learning.
- What is it?
- What are the benefits?
- What are the ingredients?
- What is the process?

20 minutes   Discuss and identify team norms. The Learning Coach should give teams a chance to establish their own norms.

20 minutes   Introduce the art of asking good questions. Discuss how to use questions to identify and challenge assumptions.

30 minutes   Practice session. Divide the group into pairs. Ask each pair to present personal success stories to each other.

15 minutes   Select (or assign) an Action Learning issue, challenge, or problem for each team.

30 minutes   Conduct the first Action Learning discussion. Ask each team to discuss its issue, identifying assumptions and developing questions for the first meeting with a sponsor. Typical questions include:

- What problem will this team solve?
- How does this problem or opportunity affect you?
- What's the real impact for the organization?
- What information is known? Unknown?
- What are your assumptions about the problem?
- What questions do you want to ask others?

---

5 Whys

Used in the Six Sigma methodology, the 5 whys refers to asking, five times, why something has happened in order to get to the root cause(s) of the problem or issue. This type of exercise may be helpful during the first Action Learning discussion.

---

15 minutes   Break

15 minutes   Discuss the Action Learning process in detail, including team expectations.

1 hour   Meet with Business Issue Sponsors. Give each team an opportunity to meet with its sponsor, ask questions, and discuss the scope and definition of their issue.

1 hour   Project planning and development of the Action Learning Charter: Convergence and planning are the keys here. Ask each team to consider all of the identified questions, issues, assumptions, concerns, and unknowns. Also have them identify major question areas, map the unknowns, and identify assumptions that need to be tested. Then have each team create a project plan and make individual assignments.

15 minutes   Wrap-up

Action Learning Team Charter

Team Name:

Contact Person:

Other Team Members:

Learning Coach:

Business Issue Sponsor:

Team Learning Objectives
We commit to learn together about:

We will hold each other accountable for:

We will track progress in the following ways:

We will measure success in the following ways:

Business Issue
Describe the issue and why it is important to the organization.

How does it support the organization's priorities?

Expected Business Outcomes
How does the project support our strategy?

What are the project measures?

Action Learning Team Meetings

*A*ction Learning team meetings follow a predictable pattern tied to the problem-solving phases described in chapter 4.

Meetings to Clarify the Issue or Problem

During early Action Learning meetings, team members clarify the issue, gain alignment, explore assumptions, and identify data collection requirements. Teams typically address questions such as:
- What's the real impact for the organization?
- What are the assumptions about the problem?
- What information is available? What is unknown?

Teams also complete the following tasks:
- Set the scope of the project and define team deliverables.
- Define team roles and responsibilities.
- Outline a project plan with project phases, owners, and a time line.
- Reflect on the team process and learning objectives.

Meetings to Gather Information and Generate Solutions

During these meetings, teams generate a large number of creative ideas about the problem or opportunity. Most groups must fight the temptation to rush straight to a solution. Challenging or long-standing issues require time, especially for creative solutions. Typical tasks for these meetings include:
- Consider internal and external sources of information.
- Agree on the root cause and all dependent variables.
- Brainstorm to generate ideas/solutions.
- Review ideas and different approaches.

Meetings to Evaluate the Options

During these meetings, teams take the ideas generated in previous meetings and narrow the focus. Groups typically find it difficult to come to a consensus on a smaller set of ideas. During this phase:

- Identify the top three solutions.
- Describe how each solution supports the execution of the organization's strategy and how each will benefit shareholders, customers, and employees.
- Reflect on the team process and learning objectives.

Midterm Doldrums

Teams often lose momentum midway through the Action Learning process. Team members skip meetings, miss key milestones, and question the value of the project. We call this the "doldrums" of Action Learning. The best teams address this problem head-on, with frank discussions and goal setting.

Meetings to Make a Decision and Prepare a Business Case

During these meetings, teams must engage in a decision-making process to determine their recommended solution. During this phase:

- Choose a preferred solution.
- Formulate recommendations into a business case.

Meetings to Prepare to Present Findings and Critically Reflect

Action Learning teams present their recommendations to the Executive Panel members. These presentations are opportunities to share accomplishments, results, and key learnings. Teams should prepare the following information:

- A brief problem statement
- A recommended solution and the justification for it
- A step-by-step implementation plan, indicating for each step:
  - who is responsible
  - what it will cost
  - the final output
- Required resources and budget
- Time required for implementation (GANTT chart showing a time line)
- Implications of recommended actions
- Potential return on investment if the solution is fully implemented
- What the team learned

These meetings also give team members opportunities to stop and reflect on the lessons of experience. Participants should focus on four key questions:

- What was our goal?
- What happened?
- What would we do differently?
- What did we learn?

Action Learning Feedback

During the Action Learning Process, you will have an opportunity to give feedback to and receive feedback from your peers. Receiving such rich and immediate feedback from others can be a rare experience, so take full advantage of the opportunity.

Focus on What Matters

Select an area of development that substantially impacts your daily work and your success as a leader in your organization. Review what you know about yourself, upcoming opportunities and challenges, and feedback from others, such as 360-degree feedback. Zero in on a skill or ability as listed on the next page.

- A skill relevant to your work
- Something you are willing to disclose
- An area in which you have room to develop
- Something about which you are willing to receive feedback

Define Your Issue

Describe the issue about which you wish to receive feedback on your feedback contract. (See next page.)

Clearly State Your Request

State your request for feedback. Clarify if necessary (e.g., "I'm concerned about two listening skills: interrupting and paraphrasing more accurately.")

Return the Feedback

Observe your teammates and provide feedback during the Action Learning process. Also, keep track of your observations so you'll remember them when the group debriefs at the end of the process.

Feedback

Traditional advice on feedback is based on the notion that feedback should be "given" to people. But high-impact feedback is not given; it is a dialogue.

View feedback as a process of discovery, not delivery. The goal of feedback is to help people get relevant information.

Don't dilute your message with unnecessary qualifiers like "maybe," "perhaps," and "a little."

Feedback Contract

During the Action Learning process, I would like feedback from the team about:

My team members want feedback on these topics:

Name/topic:

Name/topic:

Name/topic:

Name/topic:

Name/topic:

Name/topic:

Name/topic:

Learning Log

As you work with your Action Learning team, note what you are learning and reflect on how you can apply new skills and knowledge in your job.

My Personal Learning Objectives:

Personal Reflection
- What have I learned?
- What new insights have I gained?
- How is this experience helping me achieve my objectives?

Team Contribution
- How do I contribute to the team?
- What more could I do?
- Am I able to influence this team?
- What else do I have to offer?

Peer Feedback
What have I learned from my peers about my development goals? About my behavior change?

Application
How will I apply what I have learned?

Conclusion

In this chapter, we focused on the experience of the Action Learning team from program launch to presentations. As the team approaches the presentation and action phase, urgency and intensity are likely to increase. It's possible that team members who were disengaged during the analysis phase will reengage. Like other areas of life, there is nothing as motivating as a looming deadline.

As the teams prepare their recommendations, they are one critical step closer to action. As important as the work has been up to now, the ultimate impact of the Action Learning experience for both the participant and the organization depends on what happens next. As Goethe said, "Knowing is not enough; we must apply. Willing is not enough; we must do." In Chapter 6, the case for action in Action Learning will be made.

6

Where Is the Action in Action Learning?

Eric's report to the executive committee was just as James had suggested, short and to the point.

"Our teams are meeting as scheduled," began Eric. "They use structured analysis tools and processes, and have surfaced a variety of recommendations along with a business case for their ideas. Several teams actively consult their sponsors. Overall, the teams are enthusiastic about the process, even the teams that have been challenged to define and scope their project more precisely."

Two committee members who were Business Issue Sponsors shared their impressions.

"I'm impressed with the quality of the questions my team is asking and their desire to address underlying issues," said the first sponsor. "I told them that when they're done with this project, I have six more to assign. All we have to do is transfer everyone to my business unit!"

The second sponsor added, "I'm glad the teams are ambitious. But sometimes they think we can just snap our fingers and change the world. This will be a good learning experience for them if they realize what it really takes to coordinate change across our entire business."

The executive committee seemed pleased. The chairperson stated, "We appreciate that GPI is using an innovative approach to developing our high-potential managers. If Action Learning is successful, we want to know how far the approach could be extended across the firm. Come back in a few months, after the Action Learning teams give their presentations. Let us know how it's going."

Presentations

Whenever leaders empower a team to analyze an organizational problem, the time inevitably arrives when the team must account for its work and present its accomplishments. For many teams, this is the culmination of their work. Some organizations construct specific rules for these presentations, such as those used in change management methodologies. Others just take it as it comes.

Presentations are high-profile events because they have the potential either to reinforce the values of learning or to convey the message that the time spent was just an exercise. This is also a unique opportunity for all parties to demonstrate their ability to learn from each other. For example, people learn how a particular problem might be addressed, how individuals in different roles might perceive the same set of issues, and how a leadership team can embrace the insights of the Action Learning team while continuing to work with the team on the challenging issues that face the organization. In short, the presentation has the potential to be a pivotal experience.

Our view is that presentations are quite critical, but are only one point in the overall learning and change process. Presentations are where the team, the Learning

Coach, the Program Manager, Business Issue Sponsor, and the Executive Panel members converge.

The presentation, significant as it is, needs to be seen as a precursor to the next step of taking action. Even though each member of the Action Learning team may not carry out the next steps, they will have plenty of opportunities to be involved. All members of the team can solidify their learning by seeing the consequences of action and the impact of their efforts. We will come back to this point at the end of the chapter.

GPI Presentations

GPI's teams worked for several months on their projects. They defined and redefined their projects, debated the merits of project scope, and risked giving each other honest feedback about how they worked together. They were ready to share valuable insights with the Executive Panel members.

Scenario 1

The team is ready to present their recommendations on how to ensure full engagement of newly-hired graduate engineers, allowing them to appreciate the full breadth of GPI's research, engineering, and operations processes across business lines. Eric sits off to the side where he can observe without attracting attention.

The team expects to present to three Executive Panel members and representatives from the other two Action Learning teams. As people arrive, they learn that only two of the three Executive Panel members are present. The third sent a delegate from his administrative staff to take notes. The delegate has no prior experience with the Action Learning initiative. The team is disappointed with the "no show," but they proceed without a hitch. Their presentation is professional, focused, and informative.

Following the presentation, Jacques, one of the two Executive Panel members, quizzes the group. "Why did you choose this topic?"

Genevieve, the team's Business Issue Sponsor, retorts, "Didn't you read the e-mail?"

"Maybe you could refresh my memory," counters Jacques.

"I'd be happy to," snaps Genevieve. "New hires focus too much on their own silos. Within 18 months they think that their business area is the only one that matters in GPI. Once that happens, they're more likely to leave for a competitor than transfer to another business unit."

Jacques leans back in his chair. "Maybe you hire the wrong people."

Team members glance at each other and roll their eyes. Genevieve stands and faces the team. "Jacques and I will meet offline to review your recommendations in more detail."

Jacques tucks the team's presentation into his portfolio. "We'll let you know if they're feasible."

As the executives leave, Eric overhears a team member murmur, "Why bother?" Eric realizes there are serious problems, but he is at a loss as to what he could have done differently.

Scenario 2

The presentation day arrives. Eric begins the meeting with greetings and ground rules.

"Welcome to the Action Learning project update. First, I would like to acknowledge the work and commitment of the three teams, who have made great strides in their initiatives. I would also like to thank our Executive Panel members for attending and for supporting the teams from the beginning."

Jacques, an Executive Panel member, comments, "It's a good thing the COO supports development, because I rescheduled a meeting with her in order to be here."

Eric smiles. "Thank you for personally reinforcing the value of this initiative. I really appreciate it."

Jacques shrugs. "Glad to do it. She and I both agree that Action Learning is important to the firm."

Eric continues, "Today we'll hear the first team presentation. The team will briefly outline the issues, the opportunities for change, what they learned in the process, and what they believe their team and the organization can still learn by implementing the recommended actions."

Eric turns to the panel. "Please ask any and all questions that come to mind, both on the proposed recommendations and the team's insights. Also comment on what basis you could fully support implementation, or what might need to be adapted for you to support further action on the proposal."

During the presentation, Jacques interrupts, "I've seen this happen before. We have solid ideas for change, but they're not implemented. How are we going to ensure full support in a fast moving business when this region is behind plan?"

The team's sponsor, Genevieve, responds, "Jacques, even you will be impressed by their recommendations."

Jacques smiles. "If you show how this won't derail fiscal year commitments, I'll give you my full support. I'll even arrange for a briefing with the COO."

As the meeting winds down, Eric overhears two team members, Marie and Jonathan, talking. "I never knew how complex it could be to implement something across the entire region," observes Marie.

"I know," agrees Jonathan. "I had no idea how many of our business processes revolve around the fiscal calendar. Now I see why it helps to keep the calendar in front of you when you are trying to stage the introduction of new ideas!"

Marie agrees, "We just may make this work!"

Eric not only feels good about the day, he realizes that Marie and Jonathan have an entirely new level of understanding on how to work across a larger business unit.

Executive support and commitment clearly differed in the two scenarios, along with the expectations of the executives. In scenario one, disengaged executives unintentionally undermined some of the very things the Action Learning initiative sought to instill. By the time the presentation took place, it was too late for Eric to influence the process. In scenario two, Eric set and reinforced expectations about the presentations, linking the team's work with what was occurring at the meeting and what would follow. The executives and the team had a common framework for discussing action and how the learning would continue.

If action is necessary for learning to continue, then teams need to understand this expectation from the beginning. Teams need to assess their proposals for feasibility and practical implementation. They also need to create a compelling vision that addresses two issues:

- Why the proposal matters to the business. Link the current situation to the overall business need and the potential payoff.
- What the organization can learn during implementation. Indicate which unanswered questions will be addressed during implementation and what the organization stands to learn from the proposed set of actions.

When a team knows it needs to include this information in a presentation, the team and the Learning Coach can address these questions throughout their work together. Lacking this focus, the team might restrict itself to generating ideas or to grumbling about the current state of affairs. Either way, the team cannot sustain motivation over time without some commitment to real change.

A commitment to learning through action (not just generating ideas) is not only a factor for planning a presentation, it's a decision point in choosing whether Action Learning is the right approach. Had Eric realized he didn't have full executive support, as in scenario one, he might have recruited different sponsors, delayed the initiative until he had the right level of sponsorship, or sought an alternative approach to development. This is consistent with broader perspectives on change management. Action Learning as an initiative is subject to many of the dynamics that help change succeed or fail.

Hierarchy of Expected Action Taking

It may help to think of a hierarchy of action taking. Each level reflects a different degree of organizational support and each requires a different set of supporting elements to fully gain the value of Action Learning.

Level 1: Presentation Only

The presentation describes the team's proposal and learning, but there is no commitment to taking action or ongoing learning.

Risks: The team may overemphasize the problems. The feasibility of recommended actions may be secondary to problem analysis and the wish for change, leading sponsors to focus on what is missing from the recommendations rather than how they could work.

Needed support: If ongoing activity is not built into the business plan, it will be hard to sell the project despite the strength of the recommendations. The Program

Manager may have to manage the motivation of other Action Learning teams who now question the benefit of the process.

Level 2: Sponsors Agree on Action-Taking Decisions

Sponsors have clear parameters for evaluating proposals with a clear bias toward some action taking or an explicit rationale for not taking action.

Sponsors should maintain clarity on decision parameters, communicate broadly to all impacted stakeholders, and use decisions and the decision-making process as added opportunities for learning.

Level 3: Prototyping Is Part of the Process

The team understands the requirements for engaging in a prototype and they address this issue in the presentation. They also point out the additional learning they want to obtain.

The timing and feasibility of the prototype is paramount. People need to understand how the prototype impacts those outside the Action Learning team and have a plan to appropriately engage these stakeholders.

Note that across the three levels, there is a very different set of expectations for the Action Learning team, sponsors, and Executive Panel members. Note also that the primary driver or owner of the Action Learning process manages the larger set of expectations. A key part of their role is attending to communication with all stakeholders, including those participating directly in the Action Learning initiative and those who may be impacted by prototyping.

With this perspective in mind, the following pages present a set of project presentation guidelines, including an outline for a thirty-to-sixty minute presentation. This will give both teams and Learning Coaches a realistic preview of what they can accomplish during a presentation.

Project Presentation Guidelines

This outline will help you structure the presentation of your Action Learning proposal. Think of these suggestions as general guidelines, not requirements.

Introduce the Team (3 minutes)

Briefly introduce your team members, sponsor, and Learning Coach. Also acknowledge people who provided important assistance to your team.
- Team name
- Each person's name, business, and function

Make a Case for Change (5 minutes)

This is your first opportunity to make your case and "build a burning platform" for your proposed change(s).
- Start with a brief attention getter, such as an important fact or a provoking question.
- Describe the current situation. Use relevant supporting material, such as graphs, high-level data, and interview excerpts.
- Clearly state what is causing dissatisfaction in the organization. Answer the question: "Why are we unhappy with the way things are now?"
- Address potential reluctance. Demonstrate the importance of your project to your organization's strategy, vision, or values.

Present a Compelling Vision of What Could Be (10 minutes)

To persuade listeners to consider your recommendations, choose an appropriate level of detail. Too much information and your key messages will get lost in the details; too little information and you may lose credibility. As a general rule, present at the highest level while still addressing the items below. Be prepared to back up your statements with data.

Solution Overview

Briefly summarize the proposed solution. Include a statement of the solution purpose and scope, a general time frame for completion, key project members, and an overall budget with cost estimates.

Business Need

Identify and describe the business (or system) needs that will be satisfied by the proposed solution. If appropriate, describe how the initiative/change you are recommending will be integrated with ongoing work processes.

Success Measures

Define specific measures of success for evaluating the proposal; e.g., an ROI calculation. Include a deadline for attaining the goal.

Resource Estimates

Provide a realistic estimate of the required resources and costs.
- Human resource requirements, including roles, required skills, and the time commitment for each person or group
- Costs, materials, and equipment resources necessary for completing the project

Time Line

Provide a specific project time line with milestones. Include who will be accountable for each step.

Summarize, Hold an Open Dialogue, Determine Next Steps, and Conclude (7-37 minutes)

Summarize

Review your key points.

Hold Open Dialogue

Encourage questions. Prepare some prompting questions that you can use to stimulate dialogue.

Determine Next Steps

Define your bottom-line goal. Restate it in terms of go-forward steps.

Conclusion

Thank everyone and add any wrap-up comments.

> Make sure that someone on the team, if not the team as a whole, stays in contact with your Business Issue Sponsor. Test the feasibility of your proposal with your sponsor. Also practice answering potential questions.

•

Audience

A Learning Coach can enable productive reflection by asking the team to reflect on its target audience for the presentation. Discussion questions might include:

- How will the team leverage its primary sponsor for insight and advice?
- Do sponsors have agendas and concerns about proposed initiatives that cut across the organization? What are their "red flags" (e.g., timing that conflicts with key events on the fiscal calendar)?
- What is the testing period for the proposed next steps?
- What questions will be answered by implementation?
- What options are there for choosing a testing site or the scale of testing action?
- Other than the team, who needs to be involved? Who must support the next steps?
- Will the action-taking step involve the entire team or a subset of individuals? How will they coordinate the next steps?

- What continued support and action will the team request of the sponsors?
- Under what conditions would the team recommend not moving ahead with their recommendations (e.g., absence of some minimally required funding)? What would lead to early termination of action taking (e.g., unexpected restructuring of the target business unit after action has begun)?
- How will the team enable itself and the organization to capture lessons learned during the implementation phase?

Why Is Action Necessary?

Kurt Lewin confirmed, "There can be no learning without action." Action confirms whether new behavior actually makes a difference. Observation and reflection on that action confirm the extent to which new perspectives, new logic, and new routines actually matter. Action Learning teams typically call this the implementation of the team's recommendations. This action is not only the outcome of a successful team proposal, it is the place where team learning accelerates.

> *Have the team do a "dry run" of its presentation. Ask team members to play the role of sponsor and ask tough questions.*

The Program Manager has a significant communication opportunity right after the presentation. This is when he or she coordinates communication to the teams, sponsors, and the larger organization. (Hopefully the Program Manager has already communicated regularly with all stakeholders in the process.)

As events, presentations are also opportunities to celebrate and acknowledge what the teams accomplished. It's a way to provide visibility for those who committed time to the process. Also, it gives team members an opportunity to share their experience of being on a team and describe what they learned from the process.

7

What Is the Value to the Organization?

Eric Svenson worked hard to get Action Learning started at GPI. Now he is concerned that this could turn into a one-time program unless he can get outcome data that justifies the costs in terms of budget allocations and the time of key organizational leaders. While senior leaders might support the principle of Action Learning, Eric expects that they will demand more direct measures to establish value to the organization. He will need more than "happy face" evaluations to demonstrate value.

Eric lists areas to evaluate, carefully noting the financial value of each project. He notes potential cost savings of projects, recognizing that the savings will accrue over several years, even after the team completes its initial work. Eric finds it challenging to measure Return On Investment (ROI) for these types of projects. Upfront expenses are highly visible, unlike benefits, which don't materialize right away and are difficult to measure precisely. He lists what he can, and then he calls Alberto Meroni.

"Of course you should document immediate and anticipated financial benefits, but don't lose sight of the other reasons you wanted an Action Learning approach," advised Alberto.

107

What do you mean?" asked Eric.

"Action Learning is more than just another set of improvement projects. You must evaluate the learning of individuals and teams. If these high-potential team members are now better at solving business problems and they understand why it is so hard for senior executives to accomplish region-wide change, then you have demonstrated value that at least equals the financial returns of the team projects!"

Eric asked, "What impact did you see?"

"In my organization, the most notable impact was how several participants took the tools and a whole new attitude toward problem analysis back to their own work groups," continued Alberto. "Some of them got the kind of boost you don't see in regular courses or workshops. Now that's something to evaluate!"

This chapter provides Program Managers with working strategies and tools for developing an Action Learning program evaluation process. We will provide practical guidelines for showing the value of Action Learning on business results and on individual, team, and organizational learning.

Demonstrate Business Results and Learning

In many ways, Action Learning is an easy sell to senior management and HR professionals. As training budgets were squeezed in recent years, organizations significantly increased their demands that training programs show value. Because the outcome of Action Learning is a practical and tangible solution to a significant organizational challenge, senior decision makers feel there is less risk in making an investment in Action Learning. After all, even if no new learning occurs, the organization still gains something practical and tangible to show for its investment. Depending upon the nature of the project, it is quite feasible to compute a dollar value for an innovative solution developed by an Action Learning Team.

Measuring the extent and value of individual, team, and organizational learning is a different matter. Senior decision makers traditionally have been less confident that measurements of learning translate directly or indirectly to the organization's key performance indicators. Nevertheless, compelling demonstrations of the practical value of individual, team, and organizational learning can be pivotal in making the case for choosing Action Learning over much cheaper training options, such as web-based training.

Advantages to conducting a systematic assessment of the value of Action Learning include:
- Demonstrate the value of Action Learning to both the organization and individuals.
- Inform people that the program is important to the organization.
- Help ensure high-quality groups by having people focus on goals and be accountable to themselves and others.
- Capture learning from the Action Learning process.
- Provide a basis for decisions about future programs; maintain, change, or eliminate them.

How to Assess the Impact on Business Results

Assessment of business results is often appropriate and feasible because Action Learning teams focus on real business problems, and most organizations measure mission-critical performance. To assess business performance results, select performance drivers that impact future performance outcomes. For instance, if a project deliverable is a new process for handling customer complaints, an appropriate business metric might be improvement in customer satisfaction scores or a reduction in the response time to customer complaints.

In Action Learning, the business problem should be clearly defined up front. This process will include:

- Why and how the problem constrains business
- The cost to business of not developing a good solution to the problem
- How this problem relates to the mission of the organization

An Action Learning project might focus on reengineering a business process. Goals might include streamlining internal processes, reducing costs, and making the production process more efficient. In this case, measuring the benefits could require the help of the finance function. In a second example, a high-tech company might need to improve the recruiting process to raise the quality of new hires. Measuring the value of this project could require considerable organizational effort to reach consensus on the critical success factors.

Make Finance Your Friend

The finance function in the organization can help you develop a strategy for measuring the ROI for a project. When direct measures of business performance are not readily available, discuss the following questions:

- What is the impact on the organization if nothing is done? Sometimes projecting business results if everything stays the same is the most powerful way to assess the value of a deliverable.
- What is the line-of-sight between the deliverable and significant business metrics? Create a value chain between the deliverable and the ultimate benefit to the organization or the customer. This will help you identify important intervening business metrics.

Return, Risk, and Liquidity

Finance professionals evaluate value in three fundamental ways: return, risk, and liquidity. You can use these concepts to develop a comprehensive plan for measuring value in business performance.

Improve return for better performance. For example, establish that an Action Learning project created a more efficient process or reduced the cost of a product to demonstrate an improvement in return.

Reduce risk to prevent negative events, such as turnover, bad judgment, delays, flawed execution. When an Action Learning solution improves the safety or quality of a process or product, this establishes value by reducing risk.

Increase liquidity by increasing the organization's flexibility and adaptability in changing business environments. For example, if an Action Learning team developed a production innovation allowing a factory to switch production from one product line to another more rapidly, the solution would increase the liquidity or flexibility of the organization to adjust to quickly changing customer demand.

Assess the Impact on Learning

There is a problem with assessing the impact on learning. It can be very difficult to determine what individuals believe is important to learn. Many people focus on learning information or technical skills, which are certainly important to an organization. Plus, measuring comprehension and retention of information or mastery of particular technical skills is a fairly straightforward process.

However, conveying content and achieving technical mastery are rarely the goals of Action Learning. Action Learning is typically presented as an excellent way to develop high-level leadership skills (problem solving, creativity, collaborating, influencing, learning) that are very difficult to develop in traditional training formats.

To effectively assess the learning impact of Action Learning, focus on measuring changes in leadership skills. Action Learning assessment strategies must measure changes in leadership behaviors, preferably in real-world settings, rather than measure mastery of knowledge or specific technical skills.

Assess Changes in Individual Learning and Development

The first step in the assessment process occurs when team members generate individual development goals and share them with each other. In comparison to traditional training assessment protocols, which are uniform and the same for all people, individual development goals form the basis for a highly customized assessment process at the individual participant/learner level. Because each team member has different goals, the assessment focus should be tailored to each individual.

Assess through Self-Reflection. Since reflection is a core principle for Action Learning, assessment through self-reflection should be included in any comprehensive assessment process. The survey on the following pages will help in this process.

Reflection Is the Foundation for Continued Action

Your reflection should be purposeful. The goals of reflection are to:
- *Solidify your insights and make sure you remember the lessons you just learned.*
- *Identify the themes and patterns in what you do.*
- *Question and challenge your assumptions to make sure you learn the right lessons and remain open to new learning.*

Critical Reflection Improvement Survey

1 = Not at all   3 = Neutral   4 = Agree somewhat

2 = Somewhat disagree   5 = Agree strongly

Rate the extent to which you agree:					
REFLECTION					
I reflect on the way I do my work.	1	2	3	4	5
I think about my communication with my colleagues.	1	2	3	4	5
I find it difficult to pinpoint what I have learned in the past year.	1	2	3	4	5
I compare my performance with how I performed last year.	1	2	3	4	5
I compare my performance with that of my colleagues.	1	2	3	4	5
I have an accurate idea of how well I do my work.	1	2	3	4	5
CRITICAL OPINION SHARING					
I come up with ideas for how things could be organized differently.	1	2	3	4	5
I make suggestions for different working methods.	1	2	3	4	5
I share my opinions about changes at my workplace.	1	2	3	4	5
I put forth critical questions about the working of the organization.	1	2	3	4	5
I share suggestions with my colleagues about different working methods.	1	2	3	4	5

Rate the extent to which you agree:					
ASKING FOR FEEDBACK					
I discuss with my colleagues how I have developed.	1	2	3	4	5
I discuss future developments at work with colleagues.	1	2	3	4	5
If I think I have not done my work well, I discuss this with colleagues.	1	2	3	4	5
I ask my Learning Coach for feedback.	1	2	3	4	5
I ask my Business Issue Sponsor for feedback.	1	2	3	4	5
I discuss with my colleagues what I find important in my work.	1	2	3	4	5
I discuss with my colleagues our criteria for performing well.	1	2	3	4	5
CHALLENGING GROUPTHINK					
When everyone on the team is in agreement, I remain critical.	1	2	3	4	5
When I do not agree with the way a colleague does his/her work, I keep quiet.	1	2	3	4	5
I do not easily express criticism of my colleagues.	1	2	3	4	5
When I do not agree with the way a colleague does his/her work, I say so.	1	2	3	4	5
When I am the only one to disagree with the team, I keep quiet.	1	2	3	4	5
I easily submit to group decisions.	1	2	3	4	5
When I do not agree with something at work, I find it hard to say so.	1	2	3	4	5

Rate the extent to which you agree:					
LEARNING FROM MISTAKES					
If I do not know what I really should know, I try to hide the fact.	1	2	3	4	5
I do not mind making mistakes.	1	2	3	4	5
If I have not done something very well, I prefer to keep quiet about it.	1	2	3	4	5
If I make a mistake, I find it hard to forgive myself.	1	2	3	4	5
If I have not done something well, I try to forget about it as soon as possible.	1	2	3	4	5
I get embarrassed if I make a mistake.	1	2	3	4	5
SHARING KNOWLEDGE					
My colleagues are, to a certain extent, my competition.	1	2	3	4	5
I think I have the right to keep my knowledge to myself.	1	2	3	4	5
Not sharing knowledge sometimes has its advantages.	1	2	3	4	5
I enjoy helping colleagues.	1	2	3	4	5
I find it annoying when other people take advantage of my knowledge.	1	2	3	4	5
I enjoy sharing my knowledge with others.	1	2	3	4	5

Rate the extent to which you agree:					
EXPERIMENTATION					
I like to work according to tried and tested methods.	1	2	3	4	5
I feel comfortable when my work runs according to a fixed routine.	1	2	3	4	5
I do not like to deviate from the prescribed working method.	1	2	3	4	5
I like to try things out, even if it leads nowhere.	1	2	3	4	5
I experiment with other working models.	1	2	3	4	5

Assess Individual Change with a 360-degree Survey. A 360-degree feedback tool designed to measure changes in behavior over time can productively assess the impact of Action Learning at the individual level. Time2Change®, a PDI instrument, has the following advantages:

- It is efficient. It only assesses changes on the behaviors or skills that the individual has included in their individual development plan. The time "overhead" for the organization is low; the survey can usually be completed in approximately ten minutes.

- It doesn't require the same people to rate the person before and after. One of the difficulties of a typical before-and-after model is the shrinkage in the number of raters available at the end of the process because of normal organization turnover and shuffle. Time2Change® is only administered once, at the end of the process, by people who have worked with the individual for the past six months or longer. It doesn't require raters to have known the individual prior to the Action Learning process.

- Raters are only required to rate the degree of perceived change over time and are not required to remember how they rated the individual before Action Learning started.

- It avoids some of the most problematic statistical problems such as regression to the mean that plague standard pre-post assessment designs.
- It provides highly practical and understandable feedback about the degree to which changes are noticed by raters. Raters are specifically asked to rate changes in behavior, rather than the level or frequency of use of behaviors and skills (that are of questionable validity if the rater doesn't have an accurate recollection of the initial rating they gave the individual).

Two reports are available for Time2Change®: an individual report and a group report that can be created for any meaningful grouping of individuals (e.g., each team can have a report and a report can be created for all teams together).

Using a 360-degree feedback tool like Time2Change® provides another benefit for Action Learning. Recall from the discussion of the PDI Pipeline for Development® on page 12 that accountability is one of five necessary and sufficient conditions for development. By introducing the Time2Change® process at the start of an Action Learning process, the organization emphasizes the importance of accountability at the individual development level as well as the team level.

Team Assessment Strategies

Success at the Action Learning team level can be assessed externally (evaluation of the deliverable) as well as internally (the team's self-assessment of its effectiveness).

External Assessment of the Team. Assessment of the deliverable can be combined with the Action Learning team presentation to senior management. The following rating scale can be used by the audience of executives and senior managers who evaluate the final presentations. Note that the rating scales have behavioral anchors at the bottom, middle, and top positions on each scale to provide a common reference for ratings.

The Review Committee can use this assessment tool to make decisions about whether to support further development and implementation of the Action Learning team's proposals. The tool can also be used to provide feedback to Action Learning teams regarding their presentations. Teams can use this information:

- To improve the proposal if the Review Committee wants the team to continue with further development or implementation.
- During an internal briefing with the Learning Coach to deepen the team's learning.

Internal Assessment of the Team. Another approach to assessing the team's performance is to have team members evaluate the team with respect to the team success factors described earlier on pages 73-75. ••

This evaluation can be informal and based upon the questions provided in Chapter 4. Alternately, the team can use PDI's TeamTalk® questionnaire, which is based upon the TeamWise® Success Model. One advantage to using the TeamTalk® questionnaire is that the team has some useful metrics to compare performance on the six team performance factors. The TeamTalk® questionnaire can also be used periodically throughout the team's life to help it pinpoint areas for improvement in team functioning.

Assess Results at the Organizational Level

The most direct measure of results at the organizational level is changes in the organization's performance metrics.

A second approach is to seek structured feedback from key stakeholders, such as the sponsors. Here is an interview protocol you could use to evaluate both the quality of the solutions and the process used.

Sponsors Interview Protocol

Initiating the Project

- When the team proposed this issue, why did you see this as important?
- Why did you want to sponsor it?

Action Learning Team Process

- As the sponsor, how did you work with the team during the Action Learning project?
- How would you describe your role as a sponsor?
- What was your level of involvement with the team? How often did you meet with the team or interact with team members?

Results

- What were your initial reactions to the output or recommendations that the team presented to you?
- What (if anything) has happened as a result of the recommendations of the Action Learning teams?
- What do you anticipate happening? (Probe for quantitative results or critical incidents.)
- What outcomes (financial, performance, impact on employees or customers, etc.) do you expect as a result of the Action Learning team's recommendations?
- What is the value of these outcomes to you as the sponsor? What is the value to the organization?

General Comments or Suggestions

- Do you have any additional comments or suggestions?
- Would you be willing to sponsor an Action Learning project again?

Organizational Surveys. A third approach to assessing the impact of Action Learning projects at the organizational level is to survey the organization. Many organizations periodically conduct organizational climate surveys. A careful reading of the items may uncover questions that measure the success of Action Learning projects.

For instance, if an Action Learning project is designed to improve internal communications, the following questions would provide evidence for the impact of the intervention.

- How quickly are you informed when changes are made that affect your work?
- How well are people kept informed concerning what is going on throughout the rest of the organization?
- When you have questions, do you know where to get the answers?

Action Learning wouldn't change the overall pattern of survey responses, as these answers reflect the broader culture and leadership practices. However, it is reasonable to expect that participants on Action Learning teams would have different experiences of leadership, group decision making, and their potential to have an impact on the success of the business.

One prerequisite for being selected to join an Action Learning team is to be viewed as a high-performing individual, if not high potential. Therefore, members of an Action Learning team represent a valuable talent pool within the company. Significant change in the opinions of this group will capture the attention of executive stakeholders.

Sample Plan for Post-Action Learning Evaluation

The following sample plan can help Program Managers develop a comprehensive Action Learning evaluation process. The goals of this assessment process are:

- To understand and evaluate the business results of Action Learning projects, and report back to organization and team.
- To measure change in skills via a Level-2 evaluation, such as PDI's Time2Change®, and provide as feedback to individuals.•

- Generate group reports that assess overall improvement in individual skills. This information can be provided to the organization as evidence of improved learning and skill development. It can also target particular behaviors and skills that require further development.
- Identify lessons learned that senior leaders will find useful.
- Gather data and improvement recommendations for future Action Learning initiatives.

Step	Rationale	Tools	When
Generate individual development goals.	Focus team members on strategic learning goals.	Peer discussion groups Individual development plan	Beginning of project
Sponsors develop performance goal guidelines.	Provide teams with key expectations and metrics.	Dialogue between teams and Sponsors	Beginning of project
Assess learning at the individual level.	Provide feedback to team members and organization about changes in behavior and skills.	Critical Reflection Improvement Survey Critical Incident Technique Time2Change®	End of project
Assess team performance.	Provide feedback on team success factors.	TeamTalk® survey	Periodically during the project, and at the end
Assess team presentation to the Executive Panel members.	Provide feedback to teams regarding their performance during the presentation.	Presentation Feedback Form	After the team presentation

Step	Rationale	Tools	When
Assess business impact.	Provide measures that show how the Action Learning process benefits organizational performance.	Compute change scores or performance improvement metrics linked to project goals.	After the project, when it is reasonable to expect changes or improvements
Assess impact on the organization.	Provide assessment of other impacts on business and organization.	Sponsor interviews	End of project After project, after the benefits of the project emerge
Assess impact on broader organizational functioning.	Provide non-business performance metrics.	Organizational surveys	After project, when it is reasonable to expect changes or improvements

In a typical assessment, it may be more practical to select one or two assessment tools for each level (individual, team, and organization). For instance, you might use the Critical Reflection Improvement Survey and Time2Change® tools to assess learning at the individual level, use TeamTalk® and the Action Learning Presentation Feedback Form to assess learning at the team level, and evaluate linked performance metrics and sponsor interviews to assess the value of programs at the organizational level.

How Much Change Can You Expect?

We are huge proponents of evaluating the impact of interventions. We also recognize the importance of having a realistic view of how much measurable change is possible during the early phases of an Action Learning initiative. Some of the full benefits of action can't be assessed during the first six months or during the initial projects.

At times, some of the most significant outcomes occur outside of the project teams. For example:

- Individuals transfer learning from the Action Learning setting to other workplace settings.
- Participants initiate Action Learning-style team processes back on the job.
- Individuals maintain their network of relationships begun in Action Learning teams, and start to employ them across the organization.

Closing Thoughts

Take a practical approach to evaluating Action Learning. As you design your evaluation process, consider these key questions:

- What were the intentions and objectives of embarking upon Action Learning in this organization?
- What types of impact are most important in the eyes of each stakeholder group?

8
Postscript

*A*t the annual conference of the European OD Network, Arthur Freedman, noted expert on organizational development, introduces a panel of business leaders who implemented Action Learning across a multi-national business.

Eric Svenson steps up to the podium. "Let me tell you about a dream we had at GPI to find a better way of developing our people."

*E*ric is a composite of many clients with whom PDI has worked. Like many of our clients, Eric found that Action Learning was a journey of discovery. Action Learning became a place where individual, team, and organizational development efforts converged. It became a place where effective sponsorship gave teams opportunities to learn about leadership across boundaries. It became a place where participants experienced empowerment and the thrill of diving into the thorny issues of complex organizations.

We authors continue to be impressed with the potential of Action Learning to be a catalyst for so many productive types of activity and learning in organizations. In that spirit, we leave you with a few more questions.

125

What if:

- The most powerful elements of Action Learning became the daily experience of people in your company?
- Teams began thinking about learning together during every significant project?
- Teams routinely began to examine their assumptions?
- Managers began to view themselves as sponsors of important learning whenever they delegated work to a team?
- Leaders began to act as if their priority were to develop people through work and to use work to develop people's capabilities?
- The spirit of collaborative inquiry became a hallmark of your competitive advantage?

Bibliography

Adams, M.G. (2004). Change Your Questions, Change Your Life. San Francisco: Berrett-Koehler.

Argyris, C. (1982). Reasoning, Learning and Action: Individual and Organizational. San Francisco: Jossey-Bass.

Bandura, A. (1977). Social Learning Theory. Englewood Cliffs, NJ: Prentice-Hall.

Bruner, J. (1974). The Process of Education. NY: Vintage Books.

Clark, Charles (1989). Brainstorming: How to Create Successful Ideas. Chatsworth, CA: Wilshire Book Company.

Cooperrider, David L., Whitney, Diana, Sorenson, P. (1999). Appreciative Inquiry: Rethinking Human Organization Toward a Positive Theory of Change. Champaign, IL: Stipes, LLC.

Delbecq, A.L., Van de Ven, A.H., Gustafson, D.H. (1975). Group Techniques for Program Planning. Glenview, Il: Scott, Foresman and Company.

Dilworth, R., Willis, V. (2003). Action Learning: Images and Pathway. Melbourne, FL: Krieger Publishing Company.

Freedman, A. M. (1998). Pathways and Crossroads to Institutional Leadership. Consulting Psychology Journal, 50, 3, 131-151.

Knowles, M., Holton, E., Swanson, R. (1998). The Adult Learner (5th Edition). Houston: Gulf Professional Publishing Company.

Kolb, D.A. (1984). Experiential Learning: Experience as the Source of Learning and Development. Englewood Cliffs, NJ: Prentice Hall.

Lewin, K. (1947). Frontiers in Group Dynamics II: Channels of Group Life, Social Planning, and Action Research. *Human Relations, 1*, 143-153.

Marquardt, M.J. (1999). Action Learning in Action: Transforming Problems and People for World-Class Organizational Learning. Palo Alto: Davies-Black.

Marquardt, M.J. (2004). Optimizing the Power of Action Learning: Solving Problems and Building Leaders in Real Time. Palo Alto: Davies-Black.

Marquardt, M.J. (2005a). The Unique Roles and Skills of the Action Learning Coach. Presentation at Annual Convention of the Society for Industrial/ Organizational Psychology, Atlanta: GA, April 15, 2005.

Marquardt, M.J. (2005b). Leading with Questions. San Francisco: Jossey-Bass.

Moore, C.M. (1987). Group Techniques for Idea Generation. Applied Social Research Methods Series: Vol. 9. Newbury Park, NJ: Sage Publications.

McNulty, N.G. (1979). Management Development by Action Learning. *Training Development Journal:* Volume 33, Number 3.

Revans, R. (1982). The Origins of Growth of Action Learning. Melbourne, FL: Krieger Publishing Company.

Rich, J. (2003). Brain Storm: Tap into Your Creativity to Generate Awesome Ideas and Remarkable Results. Franklin Lakes, NJ: Career Press.

Senge, P., Roberts, C., Roth, G., Ross, R., Smith, B. (1999). The Dance of Change: The Challenges to Sustaining Momentum in Learning Organizations. New York: Doubleday/Currency.

Yorks, L., O'Neil, J., Marsick,V. (2000). Action Learning: Successful Strategies for Individual, Team, & Organizational Development. Newbury Park, NJ: Sage Publications.

About ...

Personnel Decisions International (PDI)

PDI is a global human resources consulting firm with distinctive expertise in building leadership talent that provides real competitive advantage. With over 700 teammembers in 28 offices around the globe, we partner with the world's leading organizations, enabling them to make consistently effective decisions about leaders.

Using field-tested strategies, systems, and tools that are unique in the industry, we help clients identify, develop, and deploy superior leaders. Our aim is simple—the well placed confidence that your current and future leaders are distinctively stronger than the competition, resulting in sustained, superior performance.

131

The Authors

Claudia Hill

Claudia (Cori) Hill is a Senior Consultant at Personnel Decisions International (PDI) and serves as the Director of Action Learning. In addition, she is responsible for the design, development, and customization of a variety of leadership and team development training curricula.

Cori brings 19 years of experience in the design, delivery, and evaluation of strategic performance improvement interventions to her client interactions. Her specialty is the creation of high-impact development programs that target the specific performance improvement goals of client organizations.

Cori received a Bachelor of Arts degree in Economics and Statistical Analysis from Florida International University in 1989 and is currently enrolled in the University of Minnesota graduate program for Human Resource Development.

H. Skipton Leonard, Ph.D.

Skip Leonard, PDI Vice President and Executive Consultant, has over 20 years of experience helping organizations hire, retain, and develop the best executive and managerial talent. Skip also has consulted with leading companies and government agencies to manage significant and fundamental changes in organizational structure, work processes, strategy, and culture. He is especially interested in helping organizations and government agencies develop executive and management leadership and talent, build high-performing teams, and behave more adaptively, creatively, and strategically in rapidly changing market conditions.

Skip received his doctoral and undergraduate degrees in Psychology from New York University and Middlebury College. He has also completed a postdoctoral fellowship in organizational consultation. Skip is a licensed psychologist and is currently an Adjunct Associate Professor at George Mason University's graduate psychology department.

A leader in the world of consulting, he previously served as President and Fellow of the Division of Consulting Psychology of the American Psychological Association. His professional and research interests include executive leadership, the development of collaboration and teamwork in senior leadership teams, and innovative consultation practice. He was the founding editor of *Consulting Psychology Journal: Practice and Theory* published by the American Psychological Association, and has numerous publications and professional presentations to his credit.

Marc B. Sokol, Ph.D.

For over 20 years, Marc Sokol has consulted in the area of talent management. As Vice President of PDI's Development Services, he specializes in organizational effectiveness and change management, leadership development and coaching, technology implementation, service quality improvement, and training design and evaluation. His experience includes working at all levels of an organization in a wide range of industries.

Marc received his doctoral degree in Industrial & Organizational Psychology from the University of Maryland. Prior to joining PDI, Marc was a Director of Human Resource Development, where he managed all aspects of training and development. He also served as adjunct faculty to the Psychology department at Rutgers University and to the Management department at New York's Polytechnic University.

Marc's research on technological change, stress management for teams, career transitions, and organizational dynamics has been presented at national conferences and published in professional journals. In 1997 he was guest editor for *Consulting Psychology Journal's* special issue on change management. More recently he has been a keynote speaker at conferences, presenting on change management and leadership development.